CATCH

THE

UNICORN

DEMYSTIFYING
BOOK MARKETING
FOR FICTION AUTHORS

DENIS CARON

First Edition

First Edition: September 2020

Book Cover Design by *Booksmith Designs*

ISBN 978-1-7773285-0-4 (ebook)

ISBN 978-1-7773285-1-1 (paperback)

Join thousands of other self-published authors
working together to sell more books
by joining the Facebook group:

https://www.Facebook.com/Groups/WeekendPublisher/

To access the free resources
mentioned in this book sign up at:

https://www.CatchTheUnicornBook.com

TABLE OF CONTENTS

PREFACE

Book marketing was, is, and always will be, the biggest struggle for self-published authors. The thing is, once you have the knowledge and the proper set of tools, it doesn't have to be a big complicated maze.

Since Amazon opened their KDP program in 2007, the publishing game has completely changed. Now, the barrier to entry is having a computer to upload your book. Because of this, as of February 2020, 6.29 million English self-published books sit on their platform, many of them not making sales. You could say they're in the deep dark basement of Amazon just collecting dust. The problem is that having your book available doesn't mean someone will find it, let alone shell out money for it.

Yes, you pay royalties to Amazon, but they deserve it. After all, they bring people. It's OUR job to prove our writing is worth reading and to capture these people as customers/new fans. And there is a way to do this without resorting to shock tactics like strutting about naked with a peacock's feather tied to your rump, waving a sign saying, "Look at me!" I am going to show you exactly how!

Throughout this book, we'll be following Jane Writer on her journey from a writer just having proudly finished her first book to a successful best-selling author earning thousands of dollars a month. Jane, now in her mid-40s, has finally pursued her lifelong dream of writing a book. She, like many others before her, second-guessed her writing and needed to expand her mind and think past just selling a few books here and there. She and her books are fictional, but her story follows the proven path that thousands of others have taken to earn serious moolah from their writing.

This book will be used heavily in conjunction with resources that you'll find available at www.CatchTheUnicornBook.com. The fact is, some resources are more helpful to have digitally, which is why I've included them through my website. Think of it as a large, dynamic appendix to this book.

Also, if you're like many others and digest information better by watching videos in a self-paced course format, consider upgrading to the full video course found at https://www.CatchTheUnicornBook.com/Video-Course/

Now, for a quick reality check. While the knowledge and tools I give you are simple and straight-forward, you need to accept there is hard work that needs to go into this. The solution is easy, the formula foolproof, but it won't succeed without your commitment. If you put the effort in upfront, you'll be able to achieve your best-seller dreams much more quickly and with more permanent results. This will also set you up for the future by bringing automaticity to your marketing process, exponentially reducing your work with each book you release. And who doesn't want the gift of less work, more play? We all do, so let's get started and finally make this dream a reality.

LEGEND

From time to time, I'm going to be using specific terms and acronyms standard in the book marketing space but might be unfamiliar to you. Therefore, I have included a legend here for you to refer back to. Having a good understanding of these terms will make it that much easier to navigate the marketing world like a pro, especially when communicating and collaborating with the marketing team you will create as you follow through the steps in this book.

☛ **PRO TIP:** Jot these quick definitions down on a post-it note to have them handy and save time. If you have a hard or paperback copy of this book, you can always use the post-it as a bookmark for the page you're on.

Here is your list:

CTA - Call to Action
Something (an action) that we want the reader to do. For example, leave a review, follow us on social media, or visit our website.

ROI - Return on investment
The amount you get in return on the financial investment you put in. Very important that we achieve a positive ROI when investing money into any advertising or marketing campaigns. Don't worry; there's not going to be too much math involved.

Above the fold
This refers to anything the user sees on a website before they have to scroll down.

PERMAFREE

An advanced pricing tactic for those with a larger catalog to give away a book for free with the idea of attracting new readers.

2MM

Refers to our exclusive Simple Two Method Marketing System

SM

Social media.

WHAT'S WITH THE UNICORN?

Just like dragons, werewolves, and mermaids, a unicorn is a beautiful, highly sought-after yet elusive animal, a creature you hear about through whispers but can never reach. This is how challenging many authors feel book marketing can be and why the unicorn was chosen as the symbol for the secrets I'll unveil in this book.

We're going to demystify what it takes to sell lots of books and turn your writing into a healthy business on its way to becoming an empire.

CHAPTER 1 🦄 MINDSET

YOU AND YOUR BOOK ARE GOOD ENOUGH

Jane almost failed high school English.

She always considered herself more of a storyteller, a brainstormer, an editor, rather than a writer. Every time she watched a movie, a TV show, or read a new book, she would think of ways that she would have put a spin on the story to improve it. In fact, her friends sought her review and keen eye before submitting their school assignments, and she felt so great when they excitedly reported the high marks they got back. But English class made her hate writing for herself - too many constraints, too many rules, and too much pressure. She barely scraped by with a passing grade and figured that was that.

Lacking confidence and insight, she was more comfortable hiding in the shadow of others. She never considered the possibility that SHE just might be destined to be an author herself.

But...

There was always something tugging at her on the inside, just wanting to be free and to be shared with the world. Eventually, she realized she wanted to write her own original story. She fell in love with the idea of becoming a confident author but still scoffed at the thought of going for it each time it came into her mind, convincing herself it was ridiculous and unrealistic and that she wasn't one of the lucky ones. She was sure that for her, writing could only ever be a hobby, not a career. So, she kept her boring job just like she was taught to, hoping this gnawing feeling would go away.

One day, she could ignore that voice no longer. It was time. She opened her laptop and a blank word document.

She brought her hands to the keyboard and paused. She stayed this way for a very long time, unable to make her fingers type. "Just write the first sentence," she coaxed herself, but the words wouldn't come.

With all the ideas she had, sitting down and writing suddenly felt impossible - so many ideas. Which ones were the RIGHT ones? Which ones were the BEST? Overwhelmed by the responsibility of picking "the right" options, she slammed the laptop shut and walked away. Discouraged and stressed, she continued to put off writing, deciding that this moment proved that she just wasn't made for it.

But still, her heart yearned.

Jane spent the next few months working on her confidence and self-worth. She took yoga classes, meditated, saw a personal life coach who got her eating and sleeping properly, helped her align herself better with her confidence, and found ways to be grateful for her life each day. Through this process, it became clearer and clearer that she had to try writing again. She couldn't get it out of her head. This is what her soul was calling out for. She worked up the courage while removing all the external and internal pressures she had placed on herself the first time.

There was no more timeline to work by, no worry about what ideas were good or bad, no more consideration of failure. All she wanted was just to write something for herself and the young woman inside of her who had always wanted more.

And so she sat down with her laptop another day, relaxed and happy, and suddenly, it all felt very natural. The narrative drizzled like melted butter down to her hands as her fingers connected with the keys at a record pace. The block had been removed. Before she could even grasp what had overcome her, she had finished her first book!

She was exhilarated! She had finally achieved it! Feeling amazing and proud, Jane, for the first time, considered putting her book up for sale. "This is going to sell, like wildfire! People will love it!" she imagined.

But then, just as quickly as she hit that high, a worrying flood of thoughts overcame her. "Or will they? What if they hate it? Who would want to read this? I'm a nobody. How do I get exposure for this story out in the world?" She was once again at a crossroads. Having felt on top of the world moments before and clear about her vision for her life, the return of self-doubt and insecurity again threatened to take it all away.

For many writers, this is a common origin of their own story. For others, the path, their destiny, if you will, has always been clear. Either way, when we write our first book, we all struggle with one thing.

The question of "Is my book good enough?" or even "Am I good enough?" After all, our book reflects us. It's a piece of our heart and soul poured onto sheets of paper. The fear of rejection on our first attempt is always at a critical high. It's our weakest moment in the process, make or break moments where the risk is highest that we will plunge into a deep pit of insecurity and negative self-talk. This is where we either turn around and run in the opposite direction with our tail between our legs, OR we embrace the fear and forge ahead.

I'm here to tell you to be brave, that your story is good enough, that YOU are good enough and that, most of all, you deserve this.

WHAT IF PEOPLE HATE MY BOOK?

What if I told you that a bad review from time to time is a good thing? If you had nothing but five-star reviews, nobody would believe it. We want to be able to set realistic expectations with our readers in our book description, but at the same time, we have to make peace with the fact that we are not going to please everyone. Just look at the top-rated books of all time. I'm talking 10,000 reviews with an average review of 4.9 and millions of readers. You'll find dozens or even hundreds of reviews from people that didn't enjoy it, and yet the book is still a success! The key here is that you're not aiming to entertain everybody on the planet. If you try to write for *everybody*, you will end up entertaining *nobody*.

Remember that although other potential readers will see these reviews, they will also judge the person writing them *and* with a much more critical eye when your overall rating is good. Many bad reviews will be ignored if the people writing them don't seem like the kind of people whose opinion that potential new readers would trust. In fact, bad reviews can subtly cause people to side with you and lead them to buy your book as a way to show their support. This is why you have to write for yourself.

Your storytelling will teach your readers to enjoy YOUR writing style, and that will keep you being able to produce book after book with ease, all the while being authentic to yourself. You want writing to feel good, not to become another job.

So let's talk ratings. Realistically, what you're looking for on Amazon is an average review of 4.3 or above out of 5. Why so specific? Well, the way the stars are filled in on Amazon, anything between 4.3 and 4.7, will show as 4.5 stars. Anything in this category increases your potential for more readers and, thus, more earnings.

If your book is not hitting those numbers or is very far away, don't panic. We'll discuss the challenges of that in the next chapter and what you can do to fix it.

WHAT IF MY STORY ISN'T ORIGINAL?

This is a common concern. Yes, it seems almost every story has been told, but there's a big caveat here. It hasn't been told from YOUR point of view. Some of the best-selling books were neither the best written nor the most original stories. What they had was smart marketing.

Without tackling the marketing, even the most compelling and incredible stories will sit stagnantly. This is the reality for most writers who just post their books but stop there. Can you imagine just how many unbelievable books are sitting in this Amazon basement, waiting to be discovered?

WHAT IF MY WRITING ISN'T GOOD ENOUGH?

Writing is a skill that's developed over a lifetime. As with any skill, the more you use it, the better you get at it. And the more open you are to having your work be reviewed and critiqued by professional editors, the more quickly this skill will develop into mastery.

We're going to illustrate this with a little comparison - just stay with me. Think of writing as working out at the gym and peer-review as the after-workout stretch. To get stronger (improve your writing), you have to lift weights and lift them consistently (practice writing). As you work out, your muscles grow by tearing and shortening (experience, breaking new barriers, trying new things in your writing, identifying any weaknesses). You will be able to lift heavier weights as the muscle is repaired (buffing out weaknesses) but the shortening will increase the potential of your tendons and ligaments to snap (burn-out, loss of passion, writer's block) as they now have a smaller range of motion (tunnel vision, loss of focus and identity) that your mind hasn't registered.

To keep that same range of motion (expertise, ability to build on your identity as a writer), you have to support the muscle growth by working on your flexibility contin-uously. You do this with an after-workout stretch (feed-back from others) to encourage the muscle to remember how to relax fully (remember where you started, avoid pitfalls and mistakes, refine your writing, stay humble). All successful writers employ professional editors be-cause they know the mistake of thinking you're the best you could be and trying to launch a book without one.

That's why I consistently recommend throughout this book that you keep writing. You have to work and flex this muscle.

One of my mentors, Ryan Levesque, puts it best: "[Your writing] doesn't have to be perfect; it just has to be done." I can't agree with this more. Whether you 100% believe the statement or not, you could be working on your first book for years and years with no end. There eventually has to be a time when you say, "Okay, this is my best shot. I'm going to launch it."

If you're short on cash to hire a professional editor, you are not up the creek without a paddle. Just look for a writing club near you, make relationships with other authors or editors, exchange books (or even just chapters) with someone else who you feel can give helpful and constructive feedback (ideally someone in your target audience - more on that later). If the reviewer is too cruel to your liking, find someone else. The point is, if you put in the effort, you will get value back, even from harsh feedback. As the old saying goes, it is better to try and fail than wonder what could have been.

WHAT IT TAKES TO MAKE IT FULL-TIME

Despite how difficult it was to write her first book, Jane was hooked. She wanted to keep writing. So much so that she resolved to do it full time. Her job as a social worker was fulfilling, but her dream was to be able to wake up, see the kids to school, pour a cup of tea, and write from home as she pleased.

When her first book was released, Jane told all her family and friends. She had her launch party at a local restaurant. She got them all to buy the book on Amazon and to leave a favorable review but noticed that beyond the investment from her support team of friends and family, her sales did not pick up. She was only making one or two organic sales per week. This was only bringing in a few bucks a month, barely enough to cover her cup of Starbucks every morning, let alone the cost of putting the book together. She knew that to make it a full-time career, she would need to increase her sales dramatically, but as a newbie on the author scene, she had no idea where to begin.

☛ MATH WARNING

The average annual income for a US citizen as of 2019, according to the U.S. Bureau of Labor Statistics (BLS), was $48,672. This is a decent income to survive on. To make the math easier, we're going to round it to $50,000 /year and base our numbers from eBooks priced at the average $2.99 on Amazon. There are many more variables (hard copy, paperback), but let's keep this simple.

After Amazon takes its 30% cut of our $2.99 book, we're left with 70%, or **$2.10**. Divide our $50,000 by 2.10, and we get **23,819.**

This means we have to sell 23,810 copies of our book a year at $2.99 to match that average annual income. That's 1,984 books a month or **66 books per day**!

Now don't let those numbers scare you. I simply wanted to point this out, to open your mind to the reality that to make writing a full-time career, you will need to sell thousands of books, not just one here and there. To get to a thousand sales, you need to expose your book as much as possible. How many people are we talking about, roughly? Well, it works out to be a multiple of thousands because not everyone who sees your book is going to buy it. Your reach HAS to be greater. And from a realist mindset, that means you need massive exposure.

In the next chapters, we are going to explore how getting our buyers funnel working smoothly will enable you to get to these heights.

WHAT IS MARKETING?

Marketing, in a nutshell, is all the tedious background work that goes into increasing the visibility and reach of your book. Successful marketing leads to greater sales of your book and opens the possibility of living off of your profits alone. Without this, no matter how great your book is, it won't sell, and you won't be able to leave your day job.

Marketing is tricky. It is a delicate art form that requires attention to detail to avoid losing all your money to just the marketing process alone. Just throwing your book out there in anyone's face is a reckless, flawed strategy. You'll only make people angry and spend yourself into the ground.

Because self-published authors rarely have a background in marketing, I wrote this book to help you spend the least amount of money while casting the widest possible net. This net is designed specifically to find people who are MOST LIKELY to enjoy your book, become a fan/reliable customer, and drive organic sales (get other people to read and buy your book). This is how your book will earn best-seller status.

STEP-BY-STEP INSTRUCTIONS TO FIND YOUR TARGET AUDIENCE

When you focus on everyone, you hit no one.

You have no doubt noticed a theme here. *Less is more.* Narrowing down your specific target audience instead of focusing solely on your genre is a crucial step before deciding on cover design, beta readers, and marketing.

When we market, we are looking for very specific people. Specifically, people that WILL read and buy our book. When we know who they are or are likely to be, we can then search for common patterns (needs, likes) that tie these people together and weave these patterns into the different elements of our book (design, writing, editing) to make our book appeal to them. This is what enables them to FIND your book in the first place so that they can, in fact, buy it. Simply, when someone can see themselves reflected in your book, they are more apt to buy it. Like attracts like.

On the flip side, part of this process is also to let go of what in your book appeals to *you* because it's often too far into the minute details, which bottlenecks your target audience and stifles your profit margin.

Why You Need to Define Your Target Audience

1. **Provide Information To Others On Your Team** - Providing very specific information to your cover designer, proofreader, editor, and beta readers will ensure they are much better able to give you cohesive feedback and the results that you *need* to be successful. It is the quickest way to avoid undergoing a lot of changes and revisions, reducing both the cost and time involved in these processes.

2. **Testing Purposes** - Before you can test out which cover and description to use, it's important to understand who exactly your target audience is.

3. **Your Marketing Campaigns** - Having this knowledge will help you get laser-focused on your advertising campaigns and ads.

Now, to find your target audience, we're going to be using a website that has over 2 billion monthly active users - Facebook. Ah yes, Facebook. Love it or hate it, you can't deny the vast amount of data they have on all of us. They may have more of our private information than we are comfortable with, but we can also use that to our advantage to pinpoint our target audience. Thankfully, all this data can be analyzed using tools and resources already available.

I could write a step-by-step guide on how to do it here, but, unfortunately, Facebook changes its interface on a fairly frequent basis. So, to get the most up-to-date method, please visit www.CatchTheUnicornBook.com for a video walkthrough.

CHAPTER 2 🦄 THREE ELEMENTS TO CONVERSION

Much like real estate where the primary focus is always location, location, location, marketing starts with the product itself. This is why we're first focussing on perfecting your book funnel. A book funnel primarily refers to the steps Joe Reader takes when he is looking for his next good read. There are three possible chokepoints in our buyers funnel, and they are as follows:

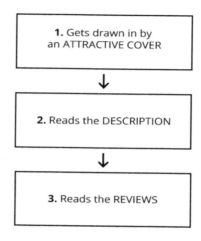

Of course, there will be readers that do not follow this sequence exactly, but the vast majority do, simply because of biology and the way it wires our eyes to our brains. For most of us, in the most basic of terms, it is a reflex to analyze things "for danger" with our eyes before we investigate closer. Humans tend to favour or be interested in specific colours, contrasts, textures, patterns, and shapes, which is why a standout cover has the power to draw us in. Next, our cognitive brain takes over and starts analyzing more intricate information (i.e., the description and the relevancy of the genre/characters to ourselves) until it has problem-solved and made a decision regarding whether to commit to the book.

We're going to be covering all three parts of the above sequence in much more detail before we get into any specific marketing tactics. I know, I know, you want to get to the juicy stuff, but if we don't talk about this first and understand each in their entirety, we run the risk of getting a low return on investment (ROI) for all of our marketing efforts.

As we go through, I'll give you different price points, resources, and tools you can use to improve all three aspects.

COVER

"Don't judge a book by its cover." **You've heard it before, but I guarantee people do and will.**

Jane didn't have a huge budget for her cover, so she tried to make it herself. She spent hours using KDP Cover Creator and Canva.com, creating mockups for her fantasy book. Finally, settling on two designs, she proudly posted them in Facebook groups to see which one people preferred.

Most comments landed towards the ones done on Canva, but overall, the comments weren't very flattering. "Outdated, not appealing, don't fit within the genre."

She took one of the more helpful comments to heart; "Your cover is the first thing Joe Reader will notice. On average, you have three seconds to make a good impression before a buyer continues scrolling down the page. It's the main piece of advertisement for your book, and when buyers see a cheaply made cover, they believe, right or not, this reflects the quality of the writing."

Finally, giving up on her brief foray into cover design, she invested in her business and her book and hired a professional.

I can't stress this enough. Having a professionally designed cover will make the marketing of your book much easier! You'll see much better returns on all of your investments (both time AND money).

When figuring out where to create the cover, these were Jane's four options.

1. Free - DIY

To be clear, I do not recommend this. Why? As we saw with Jane's case, 99% of the time, it's obvious that you did it yourself. Designing covers is an art, those who are good at it have developed their skills from education and repetition and have insider knowledge on what works. As writers, it's important to know where our strengths lie, and for most of us, it's not in graphic design.

However, although I'm reluctant to talk about this method any further, if you do choose the DIY route, I would suggest Canva.com as they have pre-made cover designs that make this process efficient. It's as easy as plug-and-play. The downfall is the potential for this to be quite time consuming as you struggle between graphics and placement of text.

This is the work that Jane did on Canva:

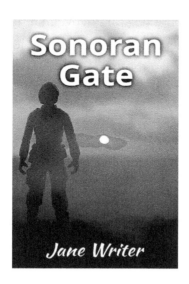

This cover reflects an amateur cover found on millions of books on Amazon. Unless you have a background in graphic design, do not waste your time trying to make your own cover. Stick with what you're good at and outsource your cover. Here are three ways at different price points to get yours done. Obviously, the higher the price, the higher the quality you can expect.

2. $ Fiverr

If you're not familiar with Fiverr, it's a gig-based system where the gig's base pricing starts at $5. A gig represents the offer that the designer makes. For example, this can be the number of cover designs or the number of formats they prepare (e.g., hardcover, kindle, etc.), or any other offer under the sun. Throughout the past decade of my online endeavours, I've purchased well over 100 gigs from different sellers on this platform, so I have a good idea of what to expect.

It can be hit-and-miss with seemingly every seller rocking 5-star reviews. There are some great people behind some of these gigs, but you can end up spending a fair amount of money just trying to find the "good one" for *you*. On the flip side, though, you can get a decent-looking cover for roughly $25. Remember to look closely at the designers' portfolios and read the reviews. You can get a good idea of what they excel in this way. You can even contact them directly if you'd like to see more of their work.

After looking through the gigs and examining portfolios of two designers, Jane gave them both a shot. She gave them both the same instructions; sci-fi with a black male protagonist in a desert camouflage who eventually leads a section of the army to another planet—a barren desert setting on a planet with three moons with a green sky.

These are what she got back:

Jane worked back and forth with both designers but wasn't able to capture the ultimate feeling of her book.

The difference between a DIY and a cover from Fiverr can be significant. However, since cover designing is an art, and with limited instructions available to give to the sellers, every designer will have their own take on it. Test out different designers and examine their portfolios carefully before ordering.

☛ **PRO TIP: ALWAYS order the source file.** This way, you can make changes with the design yourself. This is often much easier than trying to communicate back and forth with the seller.

To save more on Fiverr, visit
www.CatchTheUnicornBook.com
for a link to get 20% off your first order.

Going the Fiverr route can yield unexpectedly positive results (if you find the one diamond designer in the rough). Still, if you want a guarantee of quality, the next option is best.

3. $-$$$ Freelance Designers

You can find freelancers in many different spaces, the best places being in Facebook Groups, Upwork.com, or on Instagram. Do a hashtag search (#bookcovers, #fictionbookcovers, #fantasybookcover, etc.) with hundreds of talented (and not so talented) designs, and their creators will show up. The upside here is that designers will usually have professional pages or websites where you can easily see their body of work and their process.

Upwork (or Elance, its former name) is also a neat site in this space. Here, you can post the details of a job along with a budget, and people will bid on it, meaning that they present you with their offer, and you pay for the designer you like best. The one con with this is that you have to rely on only one person's skill and creativity. If you go this route, much like getting a tattoo designed, make sure you examine their portfolios and make an informed decision based on what you see.

Jane, still not completely happy with her covers and wanting to stand out in her categories as a quality book, found a freelance designer. After searching through Facebook groups, looking through portfolios, and contacting a few designers, she felt a connection and chose a designer. They gave her an extensive questionnaire along with instructions on how to create a Pinterest board of images that inspired her.

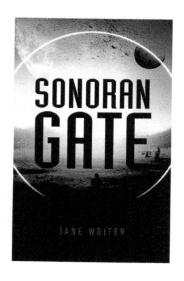

For the purposes of this book, I enlisted a working cover designer to draft an example of what a true professional can deliver. The extremely talented Claire designed the above cover. Check out her work at booksmithdesign.com.

As you can see, the main cover image is much more reflective of the feel of the story. The scene shows the protagonist about to enter the gate into the new world. His small size makes the portal and world feel huge. The moons are visible to take the cover straight to the sci-fi genre. (it features the third moon on the back cover) The low horizon line makes the scene feel vast, and the ruins in the distance give the scene depth and more of a story to discover. The title is the main focus with a rough metal texture to represent military equipment. The height of the letters in the word 'gate' evokes an epic feeling. The colours represent the land and sky but also nod to military colours.

4. $$$ 99designs

This is also a neat site in this space. An upgrade to Upwork, it's a system where you choose how much you're willing to pay the winner and multiple designers then create and submit their designs to you. The plus here is that you get to see these designs before paying for one (watermarked, to protect the designer). Obviously, the more money you're willing to pay, the better quality and larger quantity of designs you'll get.

It is on the expensive side, however, with plans ranging from $250 US to $1300, but you're almost guaranteed to get an amazing cover. Your money will be paid to the designer whose cover design you ultimately choose.

What the cover designer will need to know

- ► Page count (including front and back matter)
- ► Size of the book (i.e., 5.5 x 8.5)
- ► Your genre
- ► The way the imagery should feel
- ► Other books or images you have taken inspiration from
- ► Colours
- ► Title
- ► Cover blurb and author bio

Often, language can be an issue when trying to communicate with the designer. You want to make your instructions as clear as possible without compromising their creative sense. This can be a balancing act of detailing your wants/needs and trusting the designer. The more controlling you are about each aspect, the more difficult it will be to get a design you're happy with. My advice, focus on the mood you want to set with your cover and provide the CTA and leave the rest to them.

Head to Amazon and pick out other covers you like as examples. Remember to stay in the same genre as your book.

TEMPLATE FOR POSTING JOB ONLINE

Interviewing cover designers for my {insert your genre} book titled _____

The goal of this cover is to stand out on Amazon - as a thumbnail (appearing in search results), on the product description page, and paper.

*The imagery should make the viewer feel the book (and the author) is*_____

*I am open to any image or illustrations you choose. Here are a few words that come to mind when thinking of my book*_____

The most important part of the design is that it fits within the genre, pops off the screen, and sells.

Here are some other book covers and photos I like and have taken inspiration from (with links).

Please include the words "green pig helmet" at the top of your bid.

This last line might seem silly, but it will show you they've read your posting. This will be your first and easiest step in weeding out those who don't read and follow instructions.

DESCRIPTION

Jane felt it easy to write her book, but the 220-word limit given to her by her designer for the back flap of a 5x8" book allowed for the description was a whole other ballgame. Jane found it exceptionally difficult to summarize her entire book in so few words without it feeling like it was cheating the story and making it feel boring. After speaking with some other authors, she had connected with through Facebook, Jane was enlightened to the fact that the description could be a story all on its own, and to convert Joe Reader into a buyer, the blurb should come packed with the biggest cliffhanger of all. The cliffhanger, Jane, came to find out, is that the potential reader needs to feel like they're missing out if they DON'T read the book.

Followed closely behind the challenge of writing the book is writing the description that is going to sell the book. While there are complete books and professions dedicated to this task, we will attempt to sum it up in this section.

One of the biggest faults that people make with their book description is that it reads like a book report instead of hooking the reader in. Ask yourself, if you knew nothing about this book, would YOU feel compelled to read it?

The key here is, when we say description, we don't just mean the summary of your story. We've analyzed the top 100 fiction books on Amazon and have identified three components of a really strong book description (aka "sales pitch") right here:

Social Signal or Formal Proof

This can be a review from readers of your ARC. Usually found bolded at the very top.

The Hook

One or two sentences to immediately capture the attention of the reader

The Meat

Expand on the hook. Introduce the protaginist, the setting, end with the conflict or struggle.

Social Signal or Formal Proof

(Optional)

If you notice, the description comprises three key elements, only one of which is the story that lies between the covers. The two other components have to do with "proving" that others have both read and enjoyed the story. Let's go through them in the suggested layout sequence:

SOCIAL SIGNALS OR FORMAL PROOF

Social signals are reviews from your most validated or relatable source. Basically, they're an indicator that your book is out there, it is being seen, and it is being received well (and therefore, worth someone's time/investment). Important to note here that this should differ from a review that's already been posted for the book. In 68% of cases, the book descriptions in the study group had an average of close to two social signals or some form of formal proof.

Formal Proof about the book includes anything quantitative such as an Amazon top ranking, the number of copies sold, or any awards the book has received. If fairly new to the scene and lacking any of the former accolades, a formal proof can also be "fluff" about you (i.e., "Best-Selling Author _____ presents...", or "Author of the (book) _____ (/series) presents..."). In the study group, these social signals/formal proofs were positioned with one at the very top and the other at the bottom. In a way, they "sandwiched" the story description.

Not a best-seller yet? Don't worry, following the steps in this book will take you one step closer to being that just that.

THE HOOK

Amazon will only show readers a maximum of nine lines before having to click "read more." This is where we want the bottom of our hook to be (aka your "2-second elevator pitch"). Think about how you would sell your book to a stranger that you met in the elevator in two seconds.

The point of the hook is to capture the attention of the reader and leave them wanting more. It has to sum up the book in one or two sentences, creating a snapshot synopsis of the book, including the overall feeling of the mood and genre. It creates an emotional connection to the storyline by actively inviting the reader into the scenario and letting them consider how they would react.

Here are two examples from real best-selling books:

Dan just wanted a cup of coffee, but he never expected to find the key to a lost city served up with his latte.

or...

Judith was fine with crocheting and needlepoint, but her real hobby was murder.

THE MEAT OF THE DESCRIPTION

Now we get to the actual story. The average word count of the description in the 100 fiction books we studied was 180. The social signals, formal proof, and hook were in addition to this word count.

In the meat of the description, lead with your protagonist, the primary conflict, and the stakes. Tell them what your book is about without explaining the entire story. You've probably spent months writing all the little details, but don't leave them out. After all, we want them to be hooked on the hint of the juiciest detail, then to read the book to find out the rest.

Here are two examples from real best-selling books:

Years before, the CIA enlisted Ian to dream up terrorism scenarios to prepare the government for nightmares they couldn't imagine. Now one of those schemes has come true, and Ian is the only person alive who knows how it was done . . . and who is behind the plot. That makes him too dangerous to live.

Ian goes on the run, sweeping up an innocent bystander in his plight—Margo French, a dog walker, and aspiring singer. They are pursued by assassins and an all-seeing global-intelligence network that won't stop until Ian and Margo are dead. Ian has written thrillers like this before, but this time he doesn't know how it's going to end—or if he will be alive to find out.

or...

For years, rumors of the "Marsh Girl" have haunted Barkley Cove, a quiet town on the North Carolina coast. So in late 1969, when handsome Chase Andrews is found dead, the locals immediately suspect Kya Clark, the so-called Marsh Girl. But Kya is not what they say. Sensitive and intelligent, she has survived for years alone in the marsh that she calls home, finding friends in the gulls and lessons in the sand. Then the time comes when she yearns to be touched and loved. When two young men from town become intrigued by her wild beauty, Kya opens herself to a new life—until the unthinkable happens.

MAKING YOUR DESCRIPTION LOOK PRETTY

The easiest way to format your Book Description when your book is uploaded by going to your Amazon Author Central account. You can find a detailed video on how to do this at www.CatchTheUnicornBook.com.

☛ **PRO TIP:** Remember to change the book description for all versions you have launched. This includes your paperback, hardcover, and digital formats.

REVIEWS

Jane didn't think she could have all that much control over the reviews her readers would leave. From her own experience, she knew that there were three reasons she left bad reviews in the past: spelling/grammatical errors, inconsistency in the characters, and awkward or choppy pacing. All three elements interrupted her reading pro-

cess, knocking her out of the story and making her frustrated. An average book could have been made better if these issues were eliminated.

She knew that what her readers would be looking for is a story to get lost in, to be entertained by, and with which to escape reality. If her book had cohesive flow and was engaging with no to a minimal amount of errors, she knew she would likely earn a good review.

She figured she had a great story but still felt nervous. Would thousands of strangers find the same errors in her book? Gosh, she'd stared at her own story so long she knew she could no longer see issues herself. She joined Facebook groups looking for someone to review her book but couldn't find anyone interested enough to read her 80,000 words.

The good news is all the things that interrupt the flow of the book and drive the reader up the wall can be overcome by hiring a professional editor. Using spelling and grammar-checking software like Grammarly or ProWritingAid, even if they advertise their AI power, is still not going to beat a human touch. That's because humans read with not just their eyes and knowledge of the rules of writing, but also with their emotions, imagination, and logic.

This is where I recommend the bulk of your budget be invested. You might find someone in a FB group to read your book and give you some feedback for free. However, to be sure you will come out with quality editing, you need the expertise of a professional.

While cover design and editing will be your two biggest expenditures, there are different types of editing available, and you might not need them all.

TYPES OF EDITING
(IN ORDER FROM MOST TO LEAST EXPENSIVE)

Structural Editing (also referred to as a Developmental Edit or Overall Edit) - If you aren't entirely confident about your content, consider hiring a structural editor to improve your material organization and to suggest or draft content changes. Here, they use their skills, knowledge, experience, and unbiased judgment to educate you on what's not working in the overall story and how to fix it. This is the most expensive type of editing but can have a massive impact. Here's what they'll check for:

▶ Does the story make sense?
▶ Is everything in the right order?
▶ Is the plot plausible, and are the characters believable?
▶ How is the pacing?
▶ Is your voice compelling?

They are recommended for: anyone who is writing their first book.
Cost: This type of editing will run you approx—$ 0.08 per word (depending on the professional experience of the editor you hire).

Copy Editing (also referred to as a line edit) - Once you are confident your content is more-or-less sound, it's time to hire a copy editor. Copy editors typically also do proofreading, fact-checking, and stylistic and structural editing to ensure accuracy, consistency, completeness, and correctness. They check for:

► Grammar, spelling, punctuation, and usage.
► Consistency and continuity of mechanics and facts, including anachronisms, character names, and relationships.
► Develop a style sheet or follow one that is provided.
► Front matter, back matter, and cover copy.

Recommended for: Everyone.

Cost: $0.018 / word (depending on editor experience).

Proofreading - Your copywriter will probably be able to do proofreading to save you both time and money. Proofreaders are necessary to fix errors in spelling, punctuation, grammar, sentence structure, and word choice. They also catch continuity problems, ensure adherence to design, and check for consistency and accuracy in various elements such as cross-references and captions.

Proofreading takes place *after* editing. There is no point paying someone to proofread sections that later may be changed or removed by the copy editor. It is also not a substitute for editing.

Recommended for: Everyone.
Cost: $0.0113 / word

Beta Readers - Writers are passionate people; it is near impossible to distance yourself from something you have written emotionally and to judge your work objectively. This is where beta readers are a massive asset; they provide objective feedback on your draft manuscript. Choosing several beta readers will give you an array of changes or corrections to consider, making your story more interesting, readable, and accurate. Beta readers look over your draft to review the flow and cohesiveness, checking for plot holes, consistent characterization, and spelling and grammar issues.

Recommend for: Everyone.
Cost: Free.

☛ **PRO TIP:** The worst people to choose as your editors are your Amazon buyers. Having a disproportionate number of poor reviews could force you to remove your book and start over.

If you want to self-publish and do so successfully, beta readers, proofreaders, and copy editors are the minimum editors that you require. Yes, it will cost money, but the benefits are incomparable.

HOW TO FIND AN EDITOR

Finding someone, you feel comfortable sharing your first draft with can be a daunting and anxiety-provoking task. This might be the first time you've ever shown your work to another person. You want to find someone who will give you honest feedback in a way that helps improve your writing without tearing your confidence to shreds. **The best editors are also educators.** Here are a few ways to find someone you connect with.

Upwork - Editors set their own cost and can often give you a per hour rate that ranges from $35 - $80. Ask the editor how many words per hour they can edit, then extrapolate their per-word rate. If the $80/hr editor is considerably more experienced and faster, they may work out to be less expensive than a $50/hr editor.

Scribendi - You can get an instant quote by entering the number of works you need edited and the time frame you want the work to be completed. The best value will be for the greatest volume of words within the longest time frame. In other words, you have to pay more (especially for a large body of work) if you want the editing done, say, within a week versus a month. The downside is you don't get to interview or test out the person you hire.

Freelance - Just as with cover designers, there is a world full of talented editors working for themselves. Finding them is as easy as a Google search or by asking in Facebook groups.

Once you've gotten your feet wet here (and don't be afraid to take some time on this), select two to three potential editors that you feel you have a connection with and that specialize in your genre. Any reputable editor will give you a free sample edit of 5-7 pages. This is a great way for you and them to connect and start feeling each other out.

For a list of recommended, hand-selected freelance editors, visit www.CatchTheUnicornBook.com.

WAYS TO SAVE MONEY ON EDITING

Jane initially had sticker shock when an editor quoted her. The number was way out of her comfort zone. "Am I stuck?" she worried.

There are ways to get reduced prices on editing, but they almost always involve flexing your negotiation skills. Most services that cater to the artistic community fit well into a traditional goods market where bartering is customary. Since price is an abstract value based on both the cost boundaries that a professional has operated between as well as their own deemed self-worth, there is the flexibility to an extent, and no price is completely firm. Here are three strategies to help you get a more budget-friendly quote:

- Exchange services
  - ▷ If you have a particular set of skills that would interest the editor, negotiating trading services is one way to save money.

- Join a writing group and exchange with another writer
  - ▷ Writing groups, either physical or online, are great places to connect with other authors. While a great writer doesn't translate to a great editor, they may offer their experience and do, at the very least, some continuity editing and plot-proofing.

- Improve your writing
  - It's simple. The better a writer you become, the less editing that will be needed. Further down the line, you will also be able to remove the developmental editing all-together.

One item you will not find on this list is something that has been a growing trend lately among "influencers" online, and that is to ask for free stuff (in our case, editing) in exchange for "exposure" (aka a shout out in a very unimpressive group of their SM followers). Unless you plan to pay an editor for a long-term partnership (i.e., for a series of books) and have something of value to offer in return, do not expect any of them to give you any significant discount. It is not only insulting but also akin to theft. After all, editors are people too and have their own expenses to pay.

CHAPTER 3 🦄 MARKETING

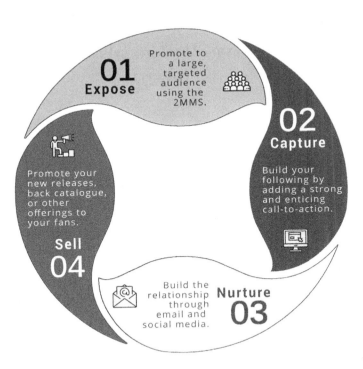

01 Expose — Promote to a large, targeted audience using the 2MMS.

02 Capture — Build your following by adding a strong and enticing call-to-action.

03 Nurture — Build the relationship through email and social media.

04 Sell — Promote your new releases, back catalogue, or other offerings to your fans.

Jane now had a great cover, a good description, and a well-edited book, but sales were still only dripping in from time-to-time. Every time a new tick on her KDP dashboard showed up, she went straight to wondering which friend or family member had bought it - not believing a stranger would be interested enough.

It's not a reflection of you as a writer. The challenge is that nobody knows you. We're going to change that in the next chapter.

The one solution to all book marketing problems is exposure.

PRICING

On Amazon, any book priced below $2.99 will get a 35% royalty payout, and anything from $2.99 - $9.99 will get a 70% royalty. Almost across the board, authors make more money in this latter sweet spot, and this is the range where I recommend *most* of your books sit.

Most of my books? You might be thinking. Let's dig deeper into this.

IF YOU HAVE ONE OR TWO BOOKS AVAILABLE

For this method, if you have only one or two books out, I strongly recommend pricing a novel or novella at $3.99 or $2.99, respectively. For a novel at a 70% royalty, this will be $2.79 profit per book, which will leave you with enough wiggle room to run profitable ads (more on this later).

Once or IF you release two or more books, this advanced method will help your books gain visibility.

MORE BOOKS, MORE ASSETS TO PLAY WITH

Much like a new song that becomes an obsession or ear-worm, when readers find a book they connect with, they will inevitably want to read more from the same author.

This is where there are advantages in having a catalogue, as it gives you more items to draw readers in and more books that are immediately available to sell to those who want to continue reading what you've written. Each available book the person hasn't yet purchased can be referred to as an upsell because they are immediate profits you can make in quantity from just one person.

In other words, the value of each reader increases the more books you have published. Once you have a larger catalogue, you have greater room to leverage a permanently free book as a way to attract more readers.

For fiction, writing books in a series is especially powerful because not only are the readers becoming attached to specific characters and worlds that you create, but they become attached to you as a writer. The only danger here is becoming "typecast," which can hinder your attempts in being successful with other books that branch away from the series. Thankfully, there are ways to combat this, including releasing books under a pen name.

GIVING BOOK 1 AWAY AS A "PERMAFREE"

What does PERMAFREE mean? Well, as the name implies, it's the digital version of your book available to download for free, permanently.

While Amazon won't allow us to set the price to zero, there is a workaround. First, post your eBook on at least one other platform. Most other significant platforms will allow you to set your price to zero. You will then have to contact Amazon and notify them of the lower competitive price, in which case they will "price match" it and set it to free on Amazon.

☛ Another math moment

When you give away a book for free, AND if the reader enjoys that work, they have the potential to purchase more of your library. Say you have ten other books out. Assuming you earn an average of $2.50 per title, that reader will be worth $25 overtime (10 books x $2.50 in royalties per book).

Understanding and taking the long view on the value of a reader can be a game-changer in how you choose to price and market your books. Think of the turtle, and the hare: slow and steady wins the race.

BOOK 2: PAID BOOK $2.99/$3.99

This could be a book in the same series or just another book from you, but the common theme here is that people will be driven to this book from your PERMAFREE option.

Book 2 can either be listed between $2.99-$3.99 to hook those readers but still take advantage of that sweet 70% in royalties.

BOOK 3 AND BEYOND: PAID BOOK, FULL PRICE $3.99+

By this time, if you've written catchy books, the readers are so invested in the story and the characters that they are dying to see what happens next and WILL buy the next book as soon as it is released (no need to read reviews when you're already hooked). Note that your books don't even have to be that good to reach this status. If you liken it to a bad tv show, after a few episodes, we are still curious to know what happens even if we think the show is dumb.

Listing all future reads after the second book as "full price" means pricing them for anything from $3.99 and higher. Usually, if your reader/potential customer is already your fan, the price is not a major deciding factor for whether they buy your book. For them, it's more the quality of the story that matters.

These numbers are fairly general, but often the length of the book also determines the value of it. For example:

▶ **Short stories** are usually priced at $0.99
▶ **Novellas** sell well at $2.99
▶ **Novels** between $3.99-$4.99 tends to be in the selling sweet spot.

The latest release can do well at $4.99 or even $5.99. Depending on sales, you can drop it down to $3.99 after six months. It is important not to become complacent once you're achieving consistent sales and just to expect that you will continue to do well. Being an author means you now own a business. A successful business will always monitor the sales data and adjust their prices to maximize their profits.

RESEARCHING AND TESTING

To get an idea of your base or starting price, you can research your genre's top 100 charts. For example, in the Mystery & Thrillers category, going above $4.99 for an indie author is difficult. Yes, you'll find some huge names in the field charging $14.99 for an eBook - but we're not there yet.

As you can probably already tell, a common theme in this book is to test continuously. When doing so, you want to keep the price you've chosen for at least 1-3 weeks, changing nothing else - not your description, not your keywords, nothing. We don't want our data muddled by other variables because then we won't know what affected our profits.

Here, you, of course, want to track sales but also mailing list sign-ups or reviews if visibility is your goal. If you're writing a series, track "read-through" rates or, in other words, the impact the sales have on the next book in the series. The further people read through or the sooner after reading one book, they push the "buy" button, the closer you're getting to the sweet spot.

EXPOSURE VS. REVENUE DEBATE

As a rule of thumb: the lower the price, the less the revenue, and the more the visibility, conversely, the higher the price, the more the revenue, but the less your visibility.

There is an advantage to having your first book for free, but there is a way for us to do this only *some* of the time. Doing it this way will give us the best of both worlds by giving us max exposure and max revenue. As part of our two-method marketing system, we will go into detail about this in the next chapter.

☛ Key Takeaways

As a *new* author, the price determines our overall revenue and visibility. Typically, the higher the price, the more reluctant a buyer is to take a chance on someone who they've never heard of before. We can remove as much of this friction as possible by giving away something for free.

CATEGORIES

When you first uploaded your book onto Amazon KDP Select, you only had the option of choosing two categories from a limited list. You can, however, have up to ten. Assigning your book in more targeted and relevant categories allows you to hit the "hot new releases" when launching. This, in turn, increases your chances of becoming a best-seller, which then leads to having more organic sales - it's a cumulative effect.

To get that coveted "best-seller" tag and to call yourself as such, you need to become the top-selling book in a category. What you need to find are relevant and non-competitive categories that your book can rank in. For example, by category analysis, if Jane just went for the category of Science Fiction-Military, she would have to sell an estimated 428 books in one day to achieve Amazon's best-seller ribbon. Alternatively, if she assigned her book into Westerns-Science Fiction, she would only need 17.

To do your research and determine what categories you can rank in, there's no better resource than K-lytics. They have taken category analysis to a whole other level with their in-depth analysis of every sub-sub-category on Amazon.

To assign your book into more than two categories, contact Amazon through your Author Central account and give them the exact category path (Books or Kindle Store > Main Category > Subcategory > Sub-Subcategory).

KEYWORDS

Amazon provides you seven fields in which to enter your keywords. I recommend you fill ALL SEVEN. The more keywords and their synonyms Amazon can associate with your book/your book meets, the higher up your book will appear when a reader types in a matching search term. The trick here is to find keywords that are relevant and popular, but not so much so that you'll be competing against the all-star players in your niche. There are manual ways to find keywords, but they're largely inefficient and waste a lot of time. Using specialized software will be much more time-efficient and accurate. This is where I recommend Publisher Rocket.

This simple software allows you to enter a seed keyword, then provides you with a list of possible keywords and estimated search volume in Amazon along with their competition score between 20-80. The lower the number, the easier it will be to compete for (rank higher). This software also comes in handy for finding keywords for Amazon ads, which we'll talk about in an upcoming chapter.

For an interview, I did with Dave Chesson, owner of Publisher Rocket, on how to best use keywords to increase your sales, visit www.CatchtheUnicorn.com.

CHAPTER 4 🦄 EXPOSURE

THE ONLY TWO METHODS YOU'LL EVER NEED TO USE

Jane knew her biggest problem was obscurity - as a first-time author; nobody knew who she was. Regardless of how good her writing or how fantastic her story, Joe Reader wouldn't care or know how much of her heart and soul she had put into this. What she needed was exposure - but not just shouting it to anybody within earshot. No, she needed a very targeted reader audience multiplied in the thousands.

The biggest problem facing self-published authors isn't plagiarism, its lack of exposure.

I'm genuinely excited to share with you the knowledge to help you sell more books. I base this entire marketing system around only two methods. They're all you need! Before we get into what they are, let's outline a few challenges Jane was up against.

☞ Budget

Money was a big concern for Jane. After paying for her cover and the editing, she didn't have the budget to spend much more money. In fact, she was looking to earn as much as she could to cover the costs she had already expended.

These methods consider financial strain, as this is the number one obstacle facing most self-published authors. If you get this part right, heck, even *half* right, you will see your exposure climb exponentially without eating away your budget.

☞ Time

With two kids, hockey practice, a full-time job, the next best-selling book in her series underway, for Jane, life was beyond busy. Sometimes, it felt like she had no time at all.

What you're good at is the writing. The more time that's available to write, the more you'll improve your craft, the more books you will publish, and the larger the catalogue you'll have for your readers. The two-method marketing approach will automatize the vast majority of your marketing process so that you lose less time marketing each time you publish a new book without compromising your potential income. This way, you can focus on the writing and let the marketing take care of itself.

☛ Effectiveness

Jane did a Google search "how to market my book" and quickly became overwhelmed by the mountains of different ideas. She asked herself, "Which ones work and which ones don't?"

If you're like Jane, you're not alone. There are dozens of different methods you could put time and money into to market your book. Book signings, guest blogging, interacting in reader groups on Facebook, giveaways, and the list goes on. I have experience doing almost all of them, and while a lot of them might sound good on paper, in the real world, they just don't work.

The key here is taking into consideration the size and relevancy of the audience. As we mentioned before, it's a numbers game. We need to get our book in front of the maximum number of qualified readers, aka the readers that are genuinely interested in your genre and would therefore actually read your book.

THE SIMPLE TWO METHOD BOOK MARKETING SYSTEM (2MM) REVEALED

So, after all this lead-up, what is this 2MM anyway? With all the criteria out of the way, the two methods that make up 2MM are **Free Book Promotions** & **Amazon Ads**.

In this chapter, we'll go into detail on precisely what these are, how to do them, why they work with our criteria, and break them down using math to show you how you can get positive ROI (return on investment) when putting them into use.

☛ The Great Pineapple on Pizza Debate: Settling the divide between KDP select and going Wide

Much like the long-heated argument over whether or not pineapple belongs on pizza, this debate has strong advocates on both sides. Before we look at the debate, we first need to define the two.

WHAT IS KDP SELECT

Amazon is the undisputed juggernaut in the publishing world, processing over 80% of all book sales online. They have the audience and the market share to offer an exclusive (or select) program to authors which they have aptly named Kindle Direct Publishing, or KDP for short. When you enroll in it, you commit the digital version of your book to them for 90 days. It means you can't sell it on any other platform, whether it be free or paid for that length of time. **What many people get confused about is that this only applies to the digital version. Paperbacks can still be made available anywhere.**

There are certain benefits to being in the KDP select program. As newbies to the scene, two of the benefits people are most interested in are the five days of free promotions and the *Kindle Unlimited page reads*. It is a monthly fee program that gives readers unlimited access to Kindle books. These readers will show up in your dashboard under the heading Kindle Edition Normalized Pages (KENP). The KENP operates differently than straight-up sales. You get paid for every page that a subscriber reads. It changes slightly every month but is usually around $0.05 for every ten pages read.

WHAT GOING WIDE MEANS

If you want to tap into the other 15-20% of the online market for eBook sales, you can publish your book on platforms such as Apple books, Google Books, and others. This means your book is now wide. As mentioned before, this is the only way to make your book PERMAFREE.

You can use one or the other - or both - just not at the same time.

The Simple Two Method Book Marketing strategy maximizes the benefits of being enrolled in the KDP Select program, and this is what we recommend you do with your first book. While this is a big decision, it's not a life-defining one. If you feel you want to explore other platforms with your digital version, you just have to wait 90 days before doing so. Often, that's how long it takes to catch our breath, anyway. After all, it is a major life accomplishment to make it to this stage, which makes it the perfect moment to sit back and feel grateful.

Now, to get down to business. 2MM is just that, two separate approaches to marketing your book. Let's explore the advantages and methodology of each to help you decide which route to take with your own book.

METHOD 1:
FREE BOOK PROMOTIONS - WHY/HOW THEY WORK

There are dozens of companies out there that have targeted subscribers and followers of over tens of thousands or even hundreds of thousands of readers who are looking for their next book. This is a veritable gold mine. This means a lot of marketing work has already been done for you (aka, the accrual of an email list).

Under this method, you apply on each site for your book to be promoted. They all have slightly different requirements, but as a standard, they want a professional cover, a minimum amount of reviews, and a minimum average review rating. Many of them require either 5 - 10 reviews (with an above 3.5 or 4-star average). After all, they want to offer only the best books to their lists.

Once you're set for a certain day, it's your responsibility to price your book accordingly for that day and they will send out their emails, their tweets, their Facebook posts, and so on.

Their followers/subscribers receive promoted free reads suggestions via these social media outlets where your book will be featured for that day. When they click the link off to your Amazon sales page they go.

To make things clear, we're only talking about your eBook here. This doesn't apply to your paperback. We couldn't give thousands of those away for free or we'd be bogged down by the printing costs.

MYTH-BUSTING

Jane thought to herself... "Why would I pay for a service to give my book away for free?" I put all of this time, money, and energy into this book. I was hoping to put this book online to actually recoup some of my money! Plus, I don't want to attract the type of reader that just wants free books all the time.

If, like Jane, you're asking yourself any of these questions, you're not alone. Throughout this section, I'll help dispel some of these common fears and misconceptions by being objective and going over real-world scenarios.

Giving something away for free is not a new concept, in fact, it's the most powerful tool we have to gain exposure.

In the business world, giving away something for free intending to attract new customers is a very common tactic and is known as a loss leader.

THE LOSS LEADER MENTALITY

Companies and people have been doing this for years. Think of inexpensive computer printers that come with starter ink cartridges. When you go to get refills, the ink is almost half the price of the printer because the initial cartridges were basically a sample size. Or even mobile games or apps that are free to download but charge you a price if you want extra features. Or cheap cruise tickets to get you on the boat then sell you $12 drinks. The list is endless. This method is popular because it works!

Of course, there are some companies and some authors who won't do this. Big names like Anne Rice, Stephen King, and the likes don't *need* to do this. They've already built their brand and name from decades of writing. We're not there yet.

We can expand our brand, our writing, and grow our list by exposing our book to a massive amount of people. The loss of leader mentality remains an effective strategy to achieve this.

But before we give away our work for free, we need to understand our objective for doing so. Here are our 6 goals for this tactic:

► Get us more reviews. The more reviews we have, the more leverage we'll have when applying to other promos; it's a cumulative effect. A good goal is to aim for 100 unique reviews. This will maximize our chances of being picked up by Bookbub (more on this coming up).

► Get more people onto our mailing list, which in turn will help us find beta readers and sell more books in the future (more on this in the next section)

► If we have more than one book out in a series, it'll help us sell more books at full price.

► If our book is in KDP Select, those readers who have Kindle Unlimited will also be reading it which will increase your page views.

► Gives us the opportunity to prove our value and brand.

► Lastly, exposure. There's no sense in keeping a dead book for sale online. When we get exposure, we're opening ourselves up to the possibility of good things happening. Remember, the biggest danger to self-published authors is obscurity. Even bad publicity is better than no publicity.

The key here is that the free product (your book) has to be high quality, otherwise the whole thing will fail. Using our previous example of printers, HP, for example, will sell a printer for below-cost to later sell us some expensive ink BUT if the printer sucks and you end up tossing it out after a few months, they're not going to make any money. The same goes for our book. We want to make it attractive with a quality cover and description, but the editing (grammar, spelling, characters, and PLOT) needs to be just as sharp, if not more so.

WHAT NUMBERS YOU CAN EXPECT TO SEE

Here's an example:

Say you have a Sci-Fi book that you promote on FreeBooksy for $75. It gets sent to 143,000 potential readers and gets 2,000 free book downloads.

Reviews. The range for reviews that you can expect is 0.3% to 0.65%. So, in this example, taking the conservative number again, using 2,000 downloads, you'd be looking at six reviews—on the low end.

With KDP Select, those readers who have Kindle Unlimited will also be reading it which will increase your page reads. A direct link to an online calculator to determine your approx. payout from page reads can be found at www.CatchTheUnicornBook.com.

If you have more than one book out, you can expect to see between a 4%-12.5% sell-through rate (aka read-through rate) in the months that follow, via promotions.

Using a sell-through rate of 4% (which is on the low end).

4% of 2000 = 80
Say the second book is priced for a reasonable $3.99.
70% cut from Amazon.
(70% x 3.99) 80 = $223.44

Not only can you make a profit, but more importantly, all of this leads to growing your list to make releasing all other books easier.

Of course, if you stack (aka combine) promo sites, you can get 5,000-10,000 downloads or even 15,000 free downloads if you get in with the king of promo sites Bookbub (more on that in its own separate section shortly).

Although these are real-world stats, not everybody is going to achieve this every time. There are a lot of factors at play here. The number of downloads can vary based on your genre, cover, description, reviews, and sometimes even current events.

WHAT KIND OF READ-THROUGH CAN YOU EXPECT AFTER THE SECOND BOOK?

This is a huge range across authors and genres. Numbers have been seen ranging on the low end of 17% all the way up to 95%. Typically, the further along they are in the series, the more invested the readers are. Relative to the earlier books in your series, you'll have fewer sales but a significantly higher read-through rate. This means that you are RELEVANT.

MARKETING WITH ONE BOOK

Jane, like every successful author before her, started out with only one book. She had heard from several people that it wasn't worth marketing until she had at least three books released. She decided to go forward anyway to build her list for book two.

Shortly after she launched Sonoran Gate, she signed up for two book promotion services; Ereader News Today (ENT) and Books Butterfly for which she paid $40 and $100, respectively. She had her book enrolled on KDP-select which allowed her to have five free-promotional days within a 90-day period. She decided to split them up and only use three days as an experiment.

Here were her results. Over the three days, she had 4,369 downloads and 38,049 page reads that continued to trickle in weeks after the promotion period. Using the calculator to estimate her earnings, she had earned approximately $177.48. She also grew her email list by 147 readers who signed up to be notified of the next book.

If Jane had had book two available priced at a reasonable $3.99 and those 150 new email subscribers had purchased it, she could have earned $418.95 extra in sales. And all this for $140 in book promotions.

But she didn't have book two available. Was it still worth it? Absolutely! She introduced thousands of readers to her writing, grew her list, and made some money through the page reads. Even if all she had achieved was to break even, the new additions to her email list were worth it.

Another option Jane had was to have a pre-order for the second book. Setting a pre-order allows customers to order your eBook as early as one year before its release date. According to Amazon, you can delay a release once for up to thirty days. If you cancel a release, there is a penalty. All the more motivation to keep you writing.

There are pros and cons to pre-orders. We'll go into more detail later in this book but in short, the pro is that you get a confirmed sale right away, a con is that it affects your book's ranking on *that* day as opposed to the day you launch. This makes it nearly impossible to get into the "hot new release" section of your categories once you do launch the finished book and therefore hinder your potential of attracting organic sales (organic, meaning ones you did not pay for).

My overall recommendation would be to have your eBook in KDP Select, include an incentive for people to sign up to your mailing list, and direct them to your website. This incentive is what we call a warm reader magnet. Cultivate that relationship by emailing them at least once a month. Then, when you release book two, you can leverage that list to sweeten your launch (more on all of this coming up).

STRATEGIES FOR BOOKING YOUR PROMOTIONS

As mentioned before, there are two ways of pricing your book for free; through KDP Select or going wide and having Amazon price match. As my recommendation would be to go through KDP Select, we're going to be focussing most of the theory on that.

We recommend splitting the five days you have available to do a free book promo into two separate chunks of time: a three-day period and a two-day period. This means you'll have a chance to run a promotion once every forty-five days (the five days of promos do not have to run consecutively).

Many promotional sites require between one week to thirty days of notice, so start booking dates well ahead of time to get the promo times right. Many sites also offer to upsell options or packages. Stick with the standard vanilla offerings; they often provide better results and value on a cost-per-download basis. There are a few exceptions, but it's difficult to keep dozens of options straight. You'll get more than enough of what you need from just the basics.

In the categories list, you'll see bronze, silver, and gold, and the one diamond recommendation. The smartest way of booking is to book a Gold promotion first, and once that is verified, attempt to book one from the silver and one from the bronze.

Want to see the categories and what they offer? Wonder which ones are best? We couldn't include an up-to-date list in this book as it changes often, so to see a current list, visit www.CatchTheUnicornBook.com.

THE ELUSIVE DIAMOND: GETTING ONTO BOOKBUB

Bookbub is a promotional site that has become the most competitive platform on which to promo your book. Paying Bookbub to feature your free book isn't cheap. It can cost you anywhere in the range of $100-$800, depending on your genre.

You might have felt some sticker shock when you read that and yes, the costs are high, but don't let that scare you. It's as close to a golden ticket as you can get. Bookbub generates 4-10 times the number of downloads of every other site combined. So, if or when you get accepted, you won't need to bother stacking it with other promotions.

What makes them such a behemoth player in the industry is their subscriber count. Again, depending on the genre, they have anywhere between 1 million – 5 million subscribers with an average free book download count of 20,000. Just like the other promotional sites, many people who have been lucky enough to get accepted have made their money back on the free deals - partly because their books are in KU, in other words, in KDP Select - and up to 3-5 times the amount they put in if they have other books in the series. If you start doing the math, this can get pretty lucrative.

There is a catch though: it's very difficult to get approved. Many people apply 10-20 times before being accepted. Their requirements are quite specific and depend on many ever-changing variables.

With that being said, here are five tips to maximize your chances:

1. Make sure you claim your author profile on Bookbub. This is a simple step. All it involves is accessing Bookbub, identifying which books are yours (then grouping them under your name), and adding an author photo and little blurb about yourself.

2. The more reviews you have, the better. Having close to 100 reviews is ideal. Keep doing free book deals to increase yours.

3. When submitting your deal, be flexible on the dates. You have the option of being flexible or choosing between a certain range. Flexibility tends to be more successful.

4. Go for the featured deal which is to set your book for free because it's easier to get in with a free deal than a $0.99 one. This is also helpful for introducing more readers to your writing because ten times more people will download your book for free than will buy it for $0.99.

5. Lastly, always write a comment during the application explaining why the book is awesome. Always fill this out with something, even if it's just one sentence as to why your book would be something their subscribers would be interested in. Also, if you have a nice review from a reputable source, it's definitely worth mentioning.

Even after following these tips, if your submission is not selected, don't fret. You can resubmit your application every four weeks. Hopefully, over the course of that time, your book will have gained even one more review and/or download which all works in your favour in the long run.

A quote from Bookbub themselves: *"[Acceptance] also depends on trends and timing factors. Our editors always look at current trends in each category when reviewing submissions. Those trends depend on what our readers have been responding to in the past few weeks AND what other books are being submitted at any given moment. Last month, WWII novels with 100 reviews might have performed best. But next month, Civil War novels with 35 reviews might be working better. This is why we always encourage authors to continue to submit. We never know how our readers' tastes will evolve over time, and the other books being submitted alongside yours are different every time."*

So, the gist of what they're saying is to keep applying and apply often. Rejection only reflects current market trends, not the quality and relevancy of your book.

☛ **PRO TIP:** While waiting to be accepted onto the Bookbub platform (mark a reminder in your calendar for every 4 weeks), keep doing other promotions, and most importantly, keep writing books.

METHOD 2: AMAZON ADS - WHY THEY'RE THE BEST KIND OF ADS FOR AUTHORS

Jane heard about Amazon ads but was too intimidated to start them. It felt complicated and math? She HATED math! But she kept reading about authors having success with them and she so desperately wanted to make writing her full-time career. At this point, she was willing to do anything to get there. She took a deep breath and relented "Fine, let's see what this is all about."

She went to the advertising site, typed in a few keywords that she thought would fit her book and sat back. Every day she checked it. Every day came up the same: no impressions. Nobody was seeing her ad! How could this be? After all, she was willing to give Amazon money for people to click on her ad. Why wouldn't they show it to people?

If you've ever tried Amazon ads and had the same, frustrating results as Jane, I'm here to tell you that all is not lost. There IS a way to fix it. Amazon ads do work, and they're not as intimidating as they seem.

In this chapter, in conjunction with exclusive resources, we'll go over what Amazon ads are, why they work, and how they're different from the more popular Facebook ads.

Amazon ads (previously known as AMS - or Amazon Marketing Service ads) allow us to advertise our books with one of two methods - **Sponsored Ads** or **LockScreen Ads**.

Sponsored Ads appear in the search results on Amazon after someone searches for the exact keywords you tell Amazon to scan for, whether they be a specific author, a book, or a phrase. They blend seamlessly into the results. So much so, that you've probably seen them hundreds of times without even noticing. The only way you can tell is by looking for the small text at the top of the result.

LockScreen Ads, on the other hand, are exactly what they sound like. When those with Kindle devices lock their screen, they're presented with an image advertising for a book. The problem is, they're not nearly as effective as sponsored ads so we will not be discussing them further.

There are plenty of reasons why Amazon ads make up the second method in our system. Here are five:

▶ **Going directly where the buyers are:** You are able to reach them while they're in buying mode. They're searching for something new to read and BOOM, there your book is, at the perfect moment, presented for their consideration.

▶ **Reaching different markets:** Until recently, you could only advertise on the .com, US-based version of Amazon BUT back in the middle of 2019, they opened up advertising to the markets in the UK, Germany, France, Italy, and Spain, along with modernizing their dashboard, which helps you see the performance of your ads in greater detail.

▶ **Find what's bottlenecking your book funnel:** By comparing your results with the benchmarks I'll set out, you can zero-in to determine if it's your cover or your description that is the weak link in your conversions.

▶ **Time commitment:** Like anything new, there will be a learning curve to using Amazon ads effectively, but it won't be as steep as other advertising platforms like Facebook. When you first set your campaigns up, I recommend you check in with them every day for about 10 mins, once they're running well.

▶ **Financial commitment:** You only pay Amazon when someone clicks on your ad. So, it could be shown to thousands of people but unless someone actually clicks on it, you won't be charged. This makes it very safe for someone looking to market their book on a budget. It's also very easy to control your budget in real-time by toggling keywords on-and-off as you discover whether or not they're working.

Here, just as with the previous tactic, having a good cover and book description will be of paramount importance. You will see lower Cost Per Clicks (CPC), more sales, and overall have an easier time making a profit when you get your description right. Again, as with other marketing techniques, the greatest advantage to your success is having more books in a series. The more books you have, the greater the chance for higher read-through-rate and profit.

FACEBOOK ADS VS. AMAZON ADS

Jane created a Facebook Author page and invited all of her family and friends to like it. She decided to boost a post. She quickly went through her $20 budget with only a few likes, no comments, and no way of knowing if any of the clicks translated into sales. With her experiment in ads complete, she was no better off in either sales or understanding of how to make the ads work for her.

How does the Amazon ad platform compare with that of Facebook? Facebook ads do get all the glamour, and I admit, they're the sexier of the two. BUT they're also far more difficult to master. There are whole courses dedicated to understanding just the basics.

Jane's experience is super common among authors. It's easy to spend lots of money before truly getting comfortable and competent enough with Facebook's ad platform to earn sales. Compare it to Amazon ads where it's a lot tougher for them to take your money. That's why I recommend playing on Amazon first - it's much safer and a great place to get your feet wet with online ads.

Still set on doing FB Ads?

If you're still set on doing Facebook ads, I suggest you look into them once you have a list of at least 1,000 email addresses. We won't get into too much detail about this but the short of it is, you can upload those email addresses to Facebook to create a custom lookalike audience. It's our way of telling Facebook to advertise to people who look like people who have been interested in and purchased your book in the past. This is where the true advertising value of Facebook lies. Without this custom audience, you're going to have to invest a lot of time and money in blind Facebook ads to see any returns.

With this being said though, you can still waste money on Amazon ads if they're not done right. Let's go over the most common mistakes first-time authors make:

COMMON MISTAKES

Improper formatting for paperback product description page: The formatting, in terms of the spacing, bolding, and italicizing text, 9 times out 10 looks nice on the eBook but is a complete afterthought on the paperback version. It's such a let-down to see nice formatting for an eBook that looks flat, at best, on the paperback. Refer back to the previous chapter about book descriptions and online resources to make sure yours looks inviting for the reader.

Not nurturing them enough: It's not just a set-it and forget-it platform; things rarely are this way. Just as I suggested marking in your calendar when you can apply to Bookbub next, mark in your calendar to check in with your campaigns for 10 mins, every day for the first week. Once you get the handle of it and your campaigns are optimized, you'll need to check-in far less often.

Not having enough keywords: Just as in Jane's example, not having enough keywords means you won't be targeting enough potential readers. You want a minimum of 200 keywords to properly test an ad campaign. Adding just 5-10, which we so commonly see, will not yield the optimal amount of impressions to note a difference. Additionally, the 5-10 that you're targeting are probably the same ones many others are, which will make them more expensive and less effective. Remember, your goal is to stand out, not to blend in. To reliably see this, you have to separate yourself from others in the genre.

TYPE OF KEYWORDS YOU NEED

There are two categories of keywords that matter to us as authors;

1. Author name and book titles (of those popular in your genre) and

2. Targeted phrases.

This means, whenever a potential reader types in "superhero fiction" or a popular book title, your book will appear in the search results for their consideration. Only when they click on it will you have to pay Amazon. The cost of the ad will be determined by the competitiveness of the keywords and the relevancy of your book. For example, if you have a romance book and you target the very popular keyword "Stephen King," your CPC or Cost-

Per-Click will be so high that you'll blow right through any conservative budget.

Which brings me to how to find your target keywords. There are two ways to collect them, manually or through paid software. Now, 200 is a large number of keywords and is definitely possible to obtain through manual labor but is SO much easier with the help of software. Let's look at how the two work.

Manually

► Found by typing in keyword phrases such as "superhero fiction" (insert whatever would match your book) into Amazon and collecting the top 40 names of authors along with the title of their book. Repeat with other relevant phrases.

► Alternately, use online resources to find other ways or synonyms around your phrases. For example, instead of "superhero fiction," you could instead use the phrase "gifted special abilities fiction."

With Software

► Enter a keyword phrase or author name into the software, click a button, and watch as dozens of potential keywords appear.

Jane purchased Publisher Rocket software and created a new campaign with 403 relevant keywords. Her impressions quickly shot up. People were attracted by her cover so they clicked on her ads. Her description hooked them in and the sales started.

The leading software in the keyword optimization industry is called Publisher Rocket.

As of the time of writing this, they require a one-time payment of $99 to sign up for access. It is VERY rare to find software that you don't pay for on a monthly basis with both user support AND regular updates. If you're serious about marketing your books, this is one of the best investments you can make (second only to this book of course).

☛ KEY TAKEAWAY:

If done incorrectly, Amazon ads can be a waste. If done right, they can be a nice and consistent source of sales that require minimal time and offer a clear ROI. To make it easy, I have available to you, for download, an exclusive, step-by-step guide to creating your ad campaign through Amazon, complete with instructional screenshots.

To access your guide, please go to www.CatchTheUnicornBook.com.

Included in the guide are:

1. Step-by-step instructions on how to create your campaign

2. A breakdown of the dashboard so you'll be clear on what's working and what's not

3. A "How To" checklist for monitoring and optimizing your campaigns

4. Troubleshooting aids for your underperforming ads

All the information in this powerful guide has been compiled from the most reputable sources, and I have personally tested each high-performing strategy through my experience running accounts for several authors. As it is my personal mission to see the underdog succeed, I've eliminated all the dead-weight and included only the strategies that really work.

THAT'S IT? BUT WHAT ABOUT ALL THE OTHER TACTICS AND STRATEGIES I'VE HEARD ABOUT?

There's no doubt that you come across dozens of different marketing strategies and tactics. While a lot of them might sound good on paper, in real life they don't work so well.

You are, of course, welcome to test out any other methods that pique your curiosity but always keep in mind the three criteria we used at the beginning of this chapter: time, money, and effectiveness.

Other ineffective strategies that I DO NOT recommend include:

▶ Newsletter swaps
▶ Book giveaways
▶ Bookbub self-serve display advertising
▶ In-person promotions or book signings

Let's look at the commonly-promoted strategy of doing a book giveaway. Yes, depending on how it's structured, a giveaway has the potential of adding to your social media following or email list but these are considered weak leads, generally attracting people who are just looking to get something for free and who are not part of your audience. These people will neither give you their money, nor a review, nor a word-of-mouth recommendation. While you would think to give away a book would automatically lead to a review, this isn't often the case. In my experience, people only review things they are truly passionate about. You also have to factor in the time it takes to run the giveaway, as well as the personal cost of ordering a copy of your own book so that you can sign it, then the added expense of shipping it to a potentially international address. It's all too much work for the return. Believe me, I have tried it...TWICE! It did not help increase my following nor my profits.

So while some strategies might seem helpful or good (when we consider our ego), they're not going to catapult you to the bestseller list. Stick with these two methods and you'll see the success that will leave you with the time you need to continue writing.

CHAPTER 5 🦄 CAPTURE

Jane believed the majority of her money was going to come from the initial sales of her book. She had heard before that she should grow her email list but always put it off, thinking it was more work than she could be bothered to do and that it seemed too simple to be an effective marketing strategy. She didn't have the foresight to see and understand that there was a potential list of buyers just chomping at the bit to learn how the story would continue and that they would most certainly give her their money if they saw a second book.

Jane wrote with purpose so it took more time to get the sequel out than she had anticipated. Not knowing when or

IF another book would come, her fans started dropping off long before the launch as they forgot about her. With that, when Jane finally released the second book, her promised sales took a nosedive and she, again, found herself having to shell out a lot of money to get her readers back.

The money is in the list. You might have heard this before, probably several times, and that's because it's TRUE. Marketing doesn't end at just selling our initial books to the maximum amount of people we cast a net over. When we sell the book to a reader, we don't truly have an author business. At this point, all we have is a singular product. If, on the other hand, we sell our book but also capture our readers' information and nurture and build our relationship with them in order to turn them into fans, THEN we have a business.

Keep in mind that people have very strong opinions about what and who they like, but they also have incredibly short memories. This is why keeping in touch with your fans and reminding them not only of who you are and the book of yours they loved but also the fact that THERE IS MORE TO COME, keeps them as potential future customers. That means all the marketing you had to do to hook them in the first place is already done for book two and beyond, for free, and with no more effort than an occasional email for the foreseeable future. Why would we want to start at ground zero ever again?

As with any business, acquiring a new customer (in our case, a reader) can cost five times more than retaining an existing one (our fanbase). This is referred to as Customer Acquisition Marketing (exposing) vs. Customer Retention Marketing (capture, nurture, and sell).

So the next question that naturally follows is how DO we capture them?

The goal of a Call-to-Action (a request for our readers to take a specific action) is to answer the question "How can we make it easy for these readers to turn into fans?" We can do this by giving them a relatively easy avenue through which to connect with us and a place to feel that they're part of a community.

The one thing that humans treasure most is feeling a personal connection with another human being. The more we feel that we know the other person, the more likely we are to feel connected as part of their like-minded community of readers, and the more we want to support the person that brought us together in the first place. This is why sending emails and/or having readers follow us on social media is SO POWERFUL. It nurtures the relationship without you ever having to personally know each fan. Most of the time, simply having brought them together in the same space allows your fans to build the community for you and your book(s).

The most common place, then, to give your fans your contact/community information is in the back matter of your book (the literal last pages of your book). In these pages, there are three Call-To-Actions (CTAs) you want to ask your reader to take.

1. Asking politely for a review

In terms of reviews, readers fall into one of three different categories;

► Those who are the serial reviewers
► Those who want to help but don't know-how
► Those who will never leave a review even if you held a gun to their heads

It's this middle group that we're targeting with this one; the readers who really enjoyed the book and want to help out in some way but don't know how to. When we tell these motivated people that reviews are helpful to us as authors, they now know what they need to do.

Here's an effective sample script that you can use in your back matter:

Thank you so much for reading [book title]! If you enjoyed the book, please consider leaving a short review on Goodreads and/or your online retailer of choice.

2. Ask them to follow you online through your social channels

For Social media, we recommend you have two outlets - the first one being Facebook, as in a Facebook Author Page, and the second one is up to you. The two most popular platforms are Instagram and Twitter. Choose whichever one you're most comfortable and familiar with. (More on how to use social media effectively in the next chapter.)

3. Magnetizing them to sign up to your email list

Although social media is being used more and more as the status-quo for communication and connection, it is paramount that you obtain an email list.

Why email and not just social media? Two words: reach and control. To really turn readers into fans, you need them on your email list so that they are easily accessible to you. We'll be discussing more what we can do with that email address and how to engage your audience in the next chapter.

I recommend that you offer an incentive in exchange for their email address. Whatever the something of value you offer, direct them to your Simple Author Website to redeem it.

THE SIMPLE AUTHOR WEBSITE

Jane knew she needed a website. Not only to show legitimacy as an author but primarily to capture her reader's email addresses. She wasn't very tech-savvy and the thought of having to create a website from scratch intimidated her.

WHY YOU NEED A WEBSITE

I understand that there might be some hesitation here, thinking that you could get by without having a website. Here are three reasons that will show you why you need one, and the limitations of using just social media.

1. Your site will act as your home base or hub on the internet. We'll be connecting all your social media pages including Facebook, Instagram, and your book, all to this one central hub. It is where we are going to be converting readers into subscribers on our email list, and then nurturing them into fans.

2. It's safe in the fact that YOU own it. You don't have to worry about algorithmic changes and you don't have to pay-to-play to reach your audience as is the case with social media. It's the one place where you can actually control your message, your branding, and in general, the whole user experience.

3. Finally, it adds legitimacy to you as an author. If it is professional looking, it is the extra little cherry that takes you from pure anonymity to projecting yourself as an established professional in the field.

TOP 4 CRITICAL ELEMENTS FOR YOUR HOME PAGE

With how far everything online has come, you need next to zero knowledge of computer stuff to be on your way. There are platforms with templates as easy as plug-and-play that you can set up in a matter of hours. The main strategy is to keep your website clean and simple so don't worry too much about design or graphics. In the vast majority of cases, simplicity, or minimalism, if you will, wins. A lot of nervousness around building a site is knowing just what to put on it. Here are the top four critical elements you need and why.

☛ First Element

Let's start off by identifying the primary function of your website – that being to capture leads (aka email addresses).

At the very top of every webpage is the hero section that is *above the fold*. The **fold** is the portion of the website the user immediately sees when they first land on your site. Think of it as the title page of your site. Here, you include your main focus or CTA (aka what action we desire the user to take). This, in our case, is for them to sign up for our mailing list.

To attract them to sign up, we need to offer something of value. Back in the "you've got mail" days, it was exciting to get emails. Now, they're much more hesitant to give away their address UNLESS they're getting something of value in return. This means we're not going to simply ask for them to sign up for our newsletter. This reader magnet needs to be compelling enough to entice people to sign up. Think back when DVDs were the hot new item. A big selling point was that you now had access to some extra features that were previously not there. This was a gold-mine to suck in new customers.

Here are some examples of what we can offer:

► Extra: Behind the scenes
  ▷ Was there some inspiration from a place you visited? How did you come up with your characters? If they really enjoyed the book, they would enjoy this.

► The preview chapter of another book, or the next book in the series:
  ▷ Yes, they could go on Amazon and read more of the second book but if they do that, we won't have their email address. According to Amazon, if your book is in KDP Select, you're able to share up to 10% of a book.

► Deleted scenes or alternate endings
  ▷ Are there any scenes or interactions between characters that didn't make the final cut?

► Character history

   ▷ Think of this as a mini prequel. Give some back-story and build out one of the characters in the book.

► Digital artwork

   ▷ These can be outsourced on Fiverr or even drawn yourself if you have a talent for that. Make it into a phone or desktop background for some extra bonus points.

► Fanfiction feature

   ▷ Once you have an established fanbase, why not feature some of your favourite fanfic that has been submitted for your series/characters? What a nice way to make your fans feel noticed and connected to you. Another way to get readers engaged in this is to offer a feature on your author website as a contest prize.

► Quizzes

   ▷ We've all seen the "Find out which character you are!" tests that follow TV series. This takes some technical know-how (that can also be outsourced to someone that knows how to do it), but this can be very engaging for your fans. It is just another way to tie people in personally with your characters and with the worlds you've created.

While this is a strong list, you're not stuck to it. Use your creativity and think of what your reader would be most interested in. You can always poll your social media followers to find out what they're interested in seeing.

Another benefit of offering these is that you're going to have a clean list of email subscribers. Those signing up for your email are those who have read your book and were interested enough to visit your site and give away their email address for some extras. This now becomes our fan list.

☛ Second Element: Library

The next element we need to include is a library of our books complete with sales page and links to each.

☛ Third Element: About the Author

Thirdly, include an "About the Author" section. Include a professional photo and a snippet about yourself and what got you writing. Include links to your social media profiles.

☛ Fourth Element: Contact

Lastly, a simple contact form for them to send you a message. Who doesn't like getting fan mail?

That's it! The beautiful thing about keeping it this simple is that it can be done all in one page. See samples of the Simple Author Website by visiting www.CatchTheUnicornBook.com.

WEBSITE SETUP PROCESS

Don't worry if you are not tech-savvy, this process is actually very straight forward but I recommend you do complete these steps in the order listed.

1. Choose a domain name - the main URL, or address for your site. For simplicity sake, most people choose their own name or their pen name. You can add pages later for each book under the main website.

2. Choose a platform. Pick one that is intuitive, user-friendly, and allows you to create and maintain your own website. Look for website platforms that are mobile-friendly, offer simple and easy-to-navigate designs, provide great templates, and are easy to update.

From my experience testing close to a dozen different platforms, your best options are either going to be:

▶ WordPress.org with a theme builder like Thrive Themes or Elementor
▶ Wix

Note that there is a difference between Wordpress.com and Wordpress.org sites – the main one being the ability to add plugins. Under no circumstance would I recommend Wordpress.com. It's going to cause you headaches with its high learning curve and minimal usability.

Overall, for the vast majority of you reading this, I recommend Wix. It's both user-friendly and easily customizable. Don't spend a lot of time making yours - one day is enough.

CHAPTER 6 🦄 NURTURE

Nurturing the relationship with our audience is the way to turn them into fans. To do this, we need a way to "touch" them. We want to keep our writing in their minds for when/if we have other books to offer them. This is where the email list comes in.

"Ughhhh. Email?" I can hear it already but there's no doubt that by every indicator of engagement, email wins over social media.

This may come as a bit of a surprise, but social media doesn't have a great engagement rate. This means everything you post won't always get to your followers!

There are complex mathematical algorithms that go into this but the gist of it is social media platforms are attention-seeking, cut-throat, and highly selective creatures; kind of like the mean girl at school. The more popular and engaging your content, the more the social media platforms will share it with your own followers. Posted a dud that only a few were interested in? They'll show it to only a small percentage of people who choose to follow you. According to optinmonster.com, the actual number of a dud post is barely over half a percent (0.58%). This means that to see all the content you post, a reader would continuously have to visit your SM home page because your posts won't automatically be programmed into their newsfeeds. And post popularity depends not only on engagement and visual-appeal but something as benign as being posted at the right time of the day.

These parameters can be challenging and cause anxiety for authors who feel they need to come out with super engaging content every day. With this being said, social media does have its place and we'll explore that shortly.

On the other end of the spectrum, an email will reach about 85% of your subscribers and has an open rate of almost 23%. Comparing that in numbers, if you have 1,000 email subscribers or 1,000 followers on your Facebook Page, you could get your message out to 230 of your fans instead of just six. And yes, only a quarter of your subscribers will open your emails. This takes many people by surprise - and that's okay. With our inboxes always flooding with junk mail, not everyone is going to read every email, every time. To make sure our super important emails get through, such as when launching a new book, we'll be emailing them several times to increase our reach.

EMAIL

Jane hated writing emails. "What do I even say?" she huffed in frustration. "Do I really need to have an email list? Can't I get by just using social media?" She spoke with several best-selling authors in Facebook groups and they all had one common regret - that they didn't start building their list soon enough. Jane relented that against her internal protests, she should follow their advice. But she didn't have time to send dozens of emails a week?! How could she ever keep up with that?

Many people, like Jane, believe it takes hours a week to keep up with emails. This isn't true. Through integrating autoresponders on your site, you can send emails on autopilot, 24 hours a day, 365 days a year. You'll be able to create it once, then let it work its magic.

There is a recommended, 4-part sequence of emails to send every person who signs up. As a reminder, we'll be getting their email address from giving away our incentive, whether that be a deleted scene or character backstory. Again, our new subscribers will automatically be entered into this sequence by a background program that you will have set up in advance.

YOUR FIRST 4 EMAILS OVERVIEW

Fill-in-the-blank templates can be found in the resource section of the website but here is an overview of what you want to send your new subscribers.

Email 1 - Delivering what you promised
Immediately deliver the incentive you promised to give them when they signed up. This should be a simple and quick email with the item attached or linked.

Email 2 - Following up
Every once in awhile, initial emails can land in the reader's spam folder. So, the next day, we want to send a

follow-up email. This shows not only that you care they received it, but that you are there to assist them in downloading and viewing it (even if it was a simple PDF).

Email 3 - Review time

After you delivered your incentive and made sure they received it, you're now in a position to ask for a review. Give detailed instructions with links on how to do so. We increase the chances of them leaving us a review if we make it as easy as possible for them.

Email 4 - Be part of the team?

Invite them to become a part of your Advanced Review Copy (ARC) team. If they accept, place or "tag" them in your email marketing system as such. They will become very important in facilitating successful launches. Again, "tagging" is all automatized for you based on how you set the program up.

HOW TO SEND EMAILS ON AUTOPILOT

Again, this whole process can be automatized - set it up once and forget about it! But you can't do this with your basic Gmail or Hotmail account. You need an email marketing service.

In terms of options out there - there are plenty. The two most popular with **free** plans are Mailchimp and Mailerlite. They both have their strengths and weaknesses, but overall I recommend Mailerlite because of the features of their free plan, the user-friendliness of their dashboard, their customer service and the price (if or when you decide to upgrade). As of this writing, they have a free plan where you can have up to 1,000 contacts and send up to 12,000 emails a month. If you've just started to create your list, or if you only have a few hundred, this is a great place to start. The free plan won't give you the fancy stuff like Custom HTML Editor, delivery by time zone, or live chat support but hey it's free. When you exceed that, or if you would like some additional features or support, you can upgrade to an inexpensive monthly plan. So, the option is there for you to grow into.

To set up your first four automated emails, go to their Automation Tab and Create a Workflow. They also have a robust help section if you get stuck.

AFTER THE FIRST FOUR

After you send them the first four messages, your readers will now receive a minimum of one email a month from you. New book releases are obvious to write about but what do we write about between the launches? Here are some topics to help you brainstorm ideas:

► Let them know of all book offerings you might have, whether they be stand-alone or the next book in the series.

► Update them on your progress with the next book. Tease them with the arc of your main characters, new ones you'll be introducing, or certain settings they'll find themselves in.

► Ask for name ideas for new characters or places.

► Let them learn what inspires you. Either a certain photo or place you visited.

Each genre will be different and you'll find what topics work best for you and your fans. The one sure-fire way to know what will resonate is simply by asking them.

To set up your monthly emails in Mailerlite, click on the Campaign tab to start writing your email.

SOCIAL MEDIA

Even though your engagement rate will be much lower relative to email, social media (SM) has its place. The biggest advantage of SM is the relationships you can build. These platforms encourage social connections and that means you get to engage, connect with, and build your own support system of *other authors*. It is also a great place to scout out professionals doing formatting, cover art, you name it. Building a relationship with these people can be the best way for you to get special discounts for their services and/or business partnerships that elevate you as a professional.

One person can competently handle two platforms but beyond that, it can get tricky. Unless you have a virtual assistant to help you maintain multiple accounts, stick with just two platforms. My recommendation is that one be Facebook. Instagram and Twitter are the other most common SM platforms among fiction authors and are relevant to the field.

MAGNETIZING PEOPLE TO FOLLOW YOU

The number one rule to getting great engagement that grows your following is to be active on your SM platforms. This means posting regularly as well as engaging with other people's posts.

☛ The 35-35-30 Rule

Managing a social media account is a bit of an art form but luckily, experts have already tested different methods of attracting subscribers and found the quick secrets that make it easy for us late joiners to get ahead. One such tip is the 30-40-30 rule which breaks down the types of content you should post to get the most traction. In this method:

► 35% [of posts] should be fun, engaging, or contain inspiring content
► 35% should be educational
► 30% should be talking about yourself and selling your book

Notice how advertising for your book(s) is actually the least common type of post? For authors, the last 30% can be pictures of you as an author at different functions, giving a shout-out to other authors or creative professionals you have business partnerships with, meeting fans, or even short videos you've taken that relate to your brand. If all we do is try to sell, nobody is going to want to follow us.

Consistency! Consistency! Consistency!

Posts need to maintain a consistent look. There are obviously experts dedicated to SM management but here are a couple of basics for **text posts**.

1. When deciding on fonts, keep your selection to 2-3 max (one serif and one sans-serif that pair nicely).

2. Set a consistent style for graphics/icons.

3. Keep the text as short as possible.

4. Choose a monochromatic, compatible colour (or image) as a background. This means that if your picture posts are mostly of old, cozy libraries, you need to stay away from neon backgrounds. These set two completely different moods and are very off-putting when paired together.

5. Unless your audience is under the age of 16, avoid any imagery, fonts, or graphic elements that look childish.

Make sure that any pictures you post look professional with good lighting, clear focus, and all use the same filter/editing. Mood is everything! Pictures of your books can have a different mood than pictures of you, but all pictures of you should complement and be consistent with one another.

☛ **PRO TIP:** Happiness sells because smiles attract. Whenever possible, insert pictures that feature the subjects (or you) smiling.

If you go the video route, clips should adhere to the strict rule of relating to your brand somehow (e.g. you at a function or answering fan questions) or show one topic of unrelated content (e.g. you jamming at your band session/other passion). What is not advisable is inserting completely random videos that break consistency such as an off-the-cuff clip of you doing a workout challenge or even funny videos of your pets. Business and personal do not mix.

Other items of value you can offer are small book snippets, a live or pre-recorded reading of a chapter, and get to know the author Q&A periods. Don't forget to remind visitors to like the post as this increases the popularity of your page and increases the chances for readers yet completely unaware of your existence to discover you.

Check out @weekendpublisher on Instagram for examples.

Because we want to keep you focused on writing and again, to stay away from fancy designs, I recommend you start your author social media account by visiting Canva.com. This is a great resource for making a quick, on-the-fly, picture and text-only posts. They have readily available, very user-friendly, and easily-customizable templates already pre-scaled for different platforms such as IG and FB. They even provide suggested font pairings and have a wide array of free images you can import.

Once you're comfortable and if you have the time to play, there are also packages available through freelance sites such as Creative Market which have pre-made IG puzzle or grid templates. These are post layouts which are stylized not just at the level of the individual post, but on the IG page as a whole. They can make your author page look extremely professional but you run the risk of appearing generic as the grids are usually designed with specific moods in mind. Another downside is that these can get costly, especially if you have to purchase an extended usage license.

If you're still struggling to find content to post, there is an unwritten rule on Instagram that you can repost anyone's photos as long as you give them credit by tagging them.

If this all feels overwhelming, don't fret. As I've said before, the biggest key is simplicity. As long as you follow the rule for the type of post and how often to make it, keeping things minimal will get you far. Be careful, social media platforms are specially designed to keep you on their platform as long as possible. This can easily take you away from your writing. Don't fall into the SM black hole and get sucked in yourself.

There is a light at the end of the social media tunnel, too. Once you have some money rolling in, hiring a virtual author assistant to manage your IG account for you is the smart way to go.

For now, I recommend taking one day to set up all of your posts for the week. If you expect to be busy, plan to be at least 2 weeks ahead on posts. This means having six posts ready to go. Use free automatic posting schedulers such as Later.com to set your posts on autopilot. The idea here is that you create your posts in the order you want them and schedule them for the days and times you want. The software will then deliver them exactly as instructed.

☛ **PRO TIP:** There is a hidden productivity opportunity in setting a posting schedule that others think smart, not hard' SM influencers already use to their advantage. Try creating a posting schedule based on theme, so that you're not spending hours trying to come up with a post. For instance, Mondays can be meme days, Tuesdays can showcase books you're reading, Wednesdays can feature something about your book, etc.

☛ **PRO TIP:** Capitalize on some free advertising by inviting fans to take a photo of where they're reading your book, and to post the photo online while using a hashtag that you create, then tagging you. This leads again to absolutely free and organic advertising for you, and to what we call positive social signals (aka positive press).

If you don't feel comfortable asking people for a photo, a less intrusive yet still effective way is to ask them a question (or give them a task) and have them post their answer in the comments. One example of this would be "Who was your favorite character and why?" or "What was your favorite scene?" Really, you can use your imagination here. A side benefit to this would be additional customer development and getting insights for your next books (e.g. what are my fans wanting to see happen to so-and-so character, what other worlds are they hoping I create, etc.)

For video walkthroughs on how to best use Instagram, visit www.CatchtheUnicornBook.com.

JOIN IN WITH COLLABS

Collaboration is key. When you are first starting to reach out to others at the same level as you, set up a collaboration where you cross-post each other's content. As a first-time author of a historical non-fiction book, you can reach out to a first-time author of a historical fiction novel and share posts that both of your audiences would enjoy. This is a fairly easy way to quickly increase your followers and engagement without being in competition.

☛ Look for the Influencers

Reach out to influencers within the platform, be genuine in your approach, capture their heart, provide links to your website and bio and ask for their help. Remember, even top influencers are real people who were once in your shoes, and often once they have achieved massive success, they are willing to give back by helping others.

But be realistic in your expectations. The #1 ranked book influencer will not reply within minutes, you might wait a month or more to even get a canned rejection.

☞ The Rise of Live Videos

Platforms such as IG and FB are encouraging live videos. So much so that they actually help you grow your pages and dramatically increase your engagement. It's not for everyone, but once you have a few under your belt, you'll become more comfortable.

☞ Your Author Photo

People like familiarity. The photo they see of you on social media should also be the same photo you use everywhere else. This is part of your author branding and although we don't get deep into branding in this book, consistency is paramount. This photo should also match your personality and your writing. For example, if you write neo-noir, a black and white photo against a brick wall would be most appropriate. Psychologically speaking, people are most attracted to and drawn towards real-life photographs of people. This means you should avoid cartoons, landscapes, and photos heavily edited with crazy Snapchat-style filters.

CHAPTER 7 ✦ SELL

Jane stuck with the two method of marketing while she was working on the second book in her series. From her action and persistence, she grew her email list to over 1,000 subscribers; over one hundred of whom were interested in becoming part of her ARC team. She knew she had a huge asset to launch her next book but didn't quite know how to implement it all.

There are two categories of what we have to sell.

▶ CATEGORY A: Books that you have already released (back catalogue or other series/stand-alone books).

We spoke about how to promote these in the previous chapter through emails.

► CATEGORY B: Books that haven't yet been launched. Launching your books the right way is what we'll be focussing on in this chapter.

BOOK LAUNCHES

☞ Your Very Own Street Launch Team

Your street launch team or scream team, whatever you want to call it, is a team of ARC readers that will act as your biggest cheerleaders and ambassadors for your book. They're your biggest fans–people who are genuinely interested in your books. Since this group of readers are your superfans, you want to treat them as the VIPs they are.

What They Do

► **Provide early reviews.** In the first module, we discussed the fact that reviews are one of the three main aspects of conversion. Your street launch team will be one essential way to get those valuable reviews, as well as increase launch-day sales. This will help kick-start Amazon's sophisticated algorithm to move your book up the ranks. As we'll see in the launch sequence, these readers should receive your book somewhere between a month or two in advance. This allows time for them to read it, give feedback and for you to complete any revisions.

► **Act as your final proofreader.** No matter how many times you've been through your manuscript or how many editors work through it, there will still lie the occasional error. As these are people who are already following your work, they are committed to the story-line and characters. That means yes, they can look for spelling and grammar issues but since they're invested in the story, they can also make small suggestions on the plot, characters, and scenes.

► Give you the **motivation** you need to get through the stressful launch stage or give you the kick in the pants you may occasionally need to stay on track with your writing.

☞ How to Find Your Teams

So, we know what they can help us with, now how do we find them? How can we make it easy for them to raise their hands up to join our team?

One way, and really the easiest way, is by email invitation. As we saw in the previous chapter, we're going to be having one of our emails in our automated email program dedicated to doing just that, creating an easy avenue for those who are interested to apply.

Alternatively, if you already have an author's Facebook page/group, an Instagram Page or other social media platform, create a post asking people to participate in your launch team. Ask for their emails so you can add them to your exclusive list. Similarly, you can ask the people who routinely comment on your posts if they would take part.

☞ Setting Expectations

Before they commit to being part of your ARC team, you have to layout your expectations. In exchange for them getting advanced copies, you'll also have some tasks for them to do. Not everyone is going to follow them but at least you're telling them up-front what their role is as a part of your team. You can do this by creating a page on your website, describing your ideal team member, listing the benefits and responsibilities of being part of the team, and asking people to sign up.

Most people love offering their opinions and being part of an elite group. Capitalize on that by letting people know they can take part in a variety of ways. In addition to leaving a review on Amazon, some of the expectations you can include are:

► Providing feedback on not only the content but also the cover design and overall style and arc of your book.

► Talk about your book on their social media, posting reviews, sharing your blog posts or photos and videos from your site, and introducing you to any influencers they know.

► Leave reviews on sites other than Amazon such as Goodreads.

Remember, however, you approach people about taking part, make sure you clearly communicate your expectations - the benefits of joining your team, the group goals, steps to success, and their individual responsibilities.

☛ Communicating with Your Launch Team

As soon as they join your team you want to send out an email thanking that new team member, explaining why reviews are important, explaining how and when they will be receiving the book, and letting them know that you welcome all feedback (positive and negative). Remind them also to save your primary contact email to avoid any future communications landing in the junk folder.

First and foremost, your launch team is a group you really need to let in on your personality. Make your interactions fun, celebrate your books, and be passionate. If you think of communicating with them as a chore, your team will too and you won't get the results you want.

Essentially, as you'll see soon, this team will be a big part of your book launches, so you want to create and maintain a personal connection with them. Create a separate email list just for them, and eventually, when the list grows big enough, you can create a Facebook group exclusively for your launch team. Still, not everyone will have Facebook so you want to keep the important communications through email. You want your team to interact not only with you but with other team members to keep up the energy and excitement of the group. One great way to build a personal connection is to schedule a live video chat using Facebook or IG.

You also want to keep them engaged between books by offering sneak peeks at your next book, launching a poll on the next cover design, or creating a discussion around a topic relating to your genre. In any way you can, validate that their continued involvement on this team is of great value to you. When they feel seen and heard, it motivates them to stay committed.

What you can do for your ARC team:

One of the ways to keep your ARC team motivated as your fanbase grows is to show your gratitude for their assistance in your success. Once your launch has happened, sending those who held on until the end a gift (i.e. merch or a signed photo of yourself, etc.) or providing them the chance to win a day with you are just two ways in which you can keep them motivated to stay on your team for the next book.

☛ Their role during launch - Reviews

Price your book at $0.99 and ask your launch team to buy your book and leave a review. This is known as a soft launch. An Amazon-verified review is a review from someone who actually purchased the book for at least $0.99 or more. This holds more weight with Amazon when it comes to their search algorithm. We will be discussing the launch sequence soon but just as a teaser, launch the book in secret for $0.99 for a few days to give them a chance to purchase and leave a review, then you can increase the price to $2.99 or $3.99, whatever you choose.

Also, ask your team to include "I received a free copy of this book from the author in exchange for an honest review" or "This review was based on a complimentary pre-release copy" as part of their review, so they don't get disqualified by Amazon. Aim for ten positive reviews in the first day or two and remember, as good as their intentions might be, not everyone who commits will actually follow through.

☛ Your First Book?

If this is your first book and you don't have an email list, you can still create a viable launch team by asking family, friends and online associates to take part. They might be super-fans in a different way - super support. Their reviews won't be as strong as a team drafted from your list of readers, but they might still be able to create invaluable reviews for you.

Use some caution here, Amazon has two Community Guidelines that apply to this. Sometime in 2017, Amazon inserted a new requirement into their Community Guidelines which states:

"To contribute to Customer features (for example, Customer Reviews, Customer Answers) or to follow other contributors, you must have spent at least $50 on Amazon.com using a valid credit or debit card in the past 12 months. Promotional discounts don't qualify towards the $50 minimum."

and...

"We don't allow individuals who share a household with the author or close friends to write Customer Reviews for that author's book."

This means you can't have your partner or whomever else living under the same roof (using the same IP address) leave a review. Amazon does say that just because someone is a friend or a social media connection, doesn't necessarily result in a review being taken down. How they determine who is a close friend and who isn't is anyone's guess, but it still doesn't mean your support system can't help. Have them leave a review on another platform such as Goodreads where there are no such rules.

☛ Delivering Your Book to Your Team

To deliver your Book to your ARC team, you could post it on Google Drive or a similar cloud-based site and send them the link in the email but if they have any trouble downloading it you could miss out on a review or be stuck having to reply to everyone to show them how to upload it to their devices.

What I would recommend is using either BookFunnel or BookSprout. They both have free or low-cost plans to allow you to easily send a secure link to each team member. They also offer custom landing pages and a variety of other handy features to help your team upload the book to their devices.

☛ Pre-orders: Yea or nay?

All retailers, whether they be Amazon, Apple Books, Google Play Books, or the like, allow pre-orders. However, all are not created equal when it comes to ranking on release day.

Excluding Amazon, all the others collect and hang on to sales numbers made during the pre-order which they register all together with release day numbers, thus providing your book with a great launch day spike.

Amazon is different. Pre-orders will not count as sales on launch day. You get a rank boost only for the day the buyer places the order. For example, say you have your book for pre-order thirty days out. If a reader buys it that day, it's going to affect your ranking on THAT day only and not on the official release day.

As a result, if you are using other platforms for your eBook or paperback, you can absolutely go ahead with pre-orders. When it comes to Amazon, I advise against it.

There are other advantages to having books on pre-order. Some authors do like to have a book on pre-order just so it gives them a hard deadline - a kick in the pants if you will. If you feel as if this would work for you, do it. A few orders might trickle in but I certainly wouldn't recommend emailing your list or advertising it at this point.

☛ Launch Day Goal

For the first thirty days of your launch, your book is considered a new release. Your launch day goal is to create a splash within that month so you can rank in the Hot New Releases section of your categories. To increase your rank, you need to sell more books and have documented page reads. You want to rank as high as possible and stay there as long as you can. Start the two method marketing a week after the release or after the initial sales from your list have begun to slow down.

THE LAUNCH SEQUENCE FORMULA

Your launch preparation starts sixty days out from launch day. While the following timeline is a good rule to follow, it's not carved in stone. This timeline acts as a great framework to work from. Find what works best for you and your audience.

60 to 30 days prior to launch

Send digital copies to your ARC team using Bookfunnel or Booksprout. Depending on the length of your book, you might need to stretch it closer to the full sixty days. Remind them you're looking for honest feedback and eventually a review on Amazon and/or Goodreads.

30 days out

Send a teaser email to your main list (those not part of your ARC team). If your cover is finalized, send a reveal; get them excited!

30 to 7 days out

Continue to make final amendments/corrections based on ARC team feedback.

7 days out

Email both lists with excerpts. This is to continue to build anticipation. Send for final proofread *(optional).*

1 to 2 days before launch day

Upload to a platform(s) (if not doing pre-orders). Email the main list one final time to reiterate the hard launch day/time.

Soft launch day

Email your ARC team. Ask for reviews and remind them to add in their review that they received their copy for advanced review. The aim is to obtain ten reviews. Politely ask your ARC team to buy the book for the prelaunch discounted price of $0.99 so that their review is classified under Amazon Verified purchase. These have proven to add more weight in Amazon algorithms. Remember, not everyone will follow through. Plan for only 10% of the total ARC team to leave a review on this day.

Hard Launch Day

Once you have ten reviews, email your main list announcing the launch. It'll be a much easier decision for them to buy your book once reviews appear on the product page.

7 days after launch

Email both lists. Thank them for contributing to a great launch. Include milestones such as sales or snippets from reviews. This will capture those who either didn't read the hard launch email, those who were on the fence, or anyone that either forgot or was too busy at the time.

14 days after launch

Optional: Use the capabilities of your email marketing provider to send an email only to those who haven't opened up any of the launch day emails. This is to try to nudge the last of your email list into at least visiting the Amazon sales page for your book. Some people like to wait and see how the book performs after launch before they invest their money.

BONUS: SHOULD YOU RE-LAUNCH?

Should You Relaunch a Dead Book?

After reading through the launch sequence formula, you might be considering relaunching yours. Amazon does allow this. Here are some reasons you might want to re-launch a dead book:

► There's been a wide gap between books in a series. Over six months is generally what we mean by a wide gap, but it would really depend on your situation and how your sales are doing. Some authors talk about rapid release where they're able to release one book a month. This is not sustainable for most people;

► To improve sell-through rate (read-through rate);

► You want to flesh out the characters and storyline more;

► You've added a lot more ARC readers;

► A chance to dump old reviews for a fresh start. This is optional as you can re-launch while maintaining all your current reviews.

Before Jane released her second book, she redid the cover, the description and added fourteen thousand words to the first book which fleshed out the characters and story-line. She kept the same title and author name and marked it as second edition when she uploaded the new copy.

She planned a new launch strategy and asked her team of ARC reviewers for a second read. Since all of them had already read the original, she didn't want to resell them copies since it was the same story, just with more depth and a higher character arc.

☛ The best time to relaunch a book that is part of a series?

The short answer is right before you add another book into the series. This will build up the momentum for the next book since your characters will be fresh on the minds of the readers and they will be anxious to see how the story continues. Depending on how much you charge for the second edition, you might get a new ASIN and require a new ISBN (always best to check with Amazon).

Relaunching can be a great choice for fixing any missteps. Also, we grow over time as writers and our writing may change altogether. As we write more and more, we become more competent and might look back at our first book and wonder what we were thinking! It is also a great way to tighten up the continuity of our story as it ensures we're writing fairly similarly through multiple books, keeping the reader locked into the same imagination space.

PUTTING IT ALL TOGETHER

Jane followed the two method marketing plan whereby she was able to expose her book to thousands of targeted readers every day. She captured their emails by offering an enticing incentive that naturally led readers to visit her simple author website and submit their emails. By nurturing those relationships through email and social media, she built her own tribe of loyal fans who were ready, willing, and able to buy any of her next books. With her business set up, she had set the foundation for success, and was able to keep on target with her writing goals. Best of all, the marketing no longer confused or intimidated her and she had so much more time to focus on the things that really mattered. Jane had finally caught the unicorn.

This book was written to help you zero in and focus only on the most important aspects of marketing with the aim of saving you money and time, reducing your stress, and helping you keep writing. After all, the best marketing tactic is for you to keep writing, release more books, and improve your craft. Remember though, this all takes time; it's a marathon, not a sprint. Follow this proven path to success and you will get there.

If you remember where we started in this book, it was under the chapter of mindset. I think it's so important to emphasize this as being the true start and base of your writing journey because, in the vast majority of cases, we are our own worst critics and our own dream killers. Writing a book when you're already stressed out is not starting off on the best foot. As part of the mindset, I want to bring you back to self-care. Before you start writing and marketing, make sure that you have the following set up, which I consider being the bare minimum of going in prepared:

► Be proud of yourself and confident in your story. Be kind and complimentary to yourself.

► If still in the initial stages, write a story that YOU will enjoy. Worry about what others think once it's finished.

► Set up some form of a support group that includes people who can relate to you in this journey (e.g. an FB group for new, as-yet unpublished writers). Actively engage with these people.

► Find 2-3 writers and/or successful entrepreneurs that you admire and aspire to emulate, follow them on SM or other platforms (e.g. seeing them speak live), and have their picture displayed somewhere where you will see it every day (physical copy or on computer wallpaper).

▶ Take 5 minutes to visualize what it will feel like when you're successful before you get to work. See it as if it were true right now. Avoid placing any conditions on it; no "ifs," "buts," or "one days."

▶ Take the time to listen to your body's signals for when it's time to take a break.

▶ Set up one reward day for yourself every week. On this day, make sure to take yourself out for a date or give yourself a gift, regardless of your productivity over the week.

▶ For the power-through people: schedule a mandatory break every 2-3 hours of writing (just to eat or even stretch your legs) OR limit your writing to a specific time of day. This will prevent fatigue, loss of interest, and avoids making writing feel like work.

▶ Take care of your health. The easiest steps are to eat properly and at regular intervals and to reserve a time for exercise (any kind will do) every day. Don't forget to drink water. Your most essential tool, the brain, is 75% water! So, have a glass before you dive into your coffee.

I have compiled a checklist for you to follow through as you progress in the book. The above is the first section of that checklist and I would argue the MOST IMPORTANT to maintain throughout your journey. The checklist summarizes the key points in the book, allows for you to track your progress in a logical timeline, and will help you continue from the right place in case you take an extended break (which might happen and is completely normal!). Please see the Resources section on the www.CatchtheUnicornBook.com webpage for the complete list, which is downloadable, fillable, and printable.

I want to thank you for taking this journey with me and wish you the best success in making your authorship dreams come true. I'd like to leave you with a quotation that has kept me going through the hard times and comes from a beloved mentor of mine, Ryan Levesque:

"You don't have to get it perfect;
you just have to get it going."

A NOTE FROM THE AUTHOR

As a fellow author, you know how vital book reviews can be. If you enjoyed and gained value from this book, an honest review at the retailer or Goodreads would be greatly appreciated.

Join thousands of other self-published authors working together to sell more books by joining the Facebook group:

https://www.Facebook.com/Groups/WeekendPublisher/

To access the free resources mentioned in this book sign up at:

https://www.CatchTheUnicornBook.com

Prefer easily digestible video lessons? Upgrade to the Catch the Unicorn Video Course by visiting:

https://www.CatchTheUnicornBook.com/Video-Course/

Made in the USA
Middletown, DE
23 September 2020